Common Problems; Common Sense Solutions

Common Problems; Common Sense Solutions

Practical Advice for Small Business Owners

By Greg Hadley

iUniverse, Inc.

New York Lincoln Shanghai

Common Problems; Common Sense Solutions
Practical Advice for Small Business Owners

iUniverse, Inc.

For information address:
iUniverse, Inc.
2021 Pine Lake Road, Suite 100
Lincoln, NE 68512
www.iuniverse.com

ISBN: 0-595-32769-9

Printed in the United States of America

Contents

PREFACE

I have not led a great army into battle. I have never been the CEO of a Fortune 50 company. I have never been elected to high public office.

That doesn't mean I haven't had some wonderful experiences. This book is about my involvement with small, privately held companies. For 24 years, my partners and I bought, operated and sold a diverse group of manufacturing companies and real estate holdings. It has also been my privilege to consult with and advise the owners and managers of many firms. During the past 14 years, I have had a professional relationship with over 110 companies. Some I have been able to help. Others I have not. Whatever the final outcome of our relationship, both my clients and I have gained some insight about operating a business. Anyone who has tried it or been charged with managing a company knows how hard this job can be. Back in the 1950's and 60's, it was pretty easy to own and operate a company. There was a stability and reliability to the ebb and flow of most businesses. Sure, mistakes were made and companies failed. But, compared with today, it was just a lot easier to start, finance and operate a business successfully and profitability. Now it is a struggle no matter how smart you are or how many advanced educational degrees you possess.

This book is intended to provide the small business owner with a series of practical, straightforward and easy to understand instructions for operating their businesses better in a number of important areas. How did this book come about? When consulting with a client, I would often find myself suggesting a course of action to deal with a specific problem. For example, it might be obvious to me that the client needed to approach a bank to seek a loan. He or she might agree with this advice but then say to me, "I have no idea how to go about implementing your suggestion. Can you show me how to do it?" This would lead to a written memo or report outlining the steps necessary to implement a specific business action. It dawned on me that if this client didn't understand the process, there were probably others who also could benefit from this information. One after another, I came across business problems that were commonly faced by the owners of many of my small business clients. I would write a monograph about the issue, tuck it into my briefcase and photocopy it for my clients as needed. After all these years, I looked at the entire body of my work and said, "I believe there is enough information here that could be valuable to a lot of small business owners I haven't even met." Thus, this book was put together.

You will note that there are no chapters related specifically to Marketing or Manufacturing issues. There is a lot of excellent information that discusses the general concepts of Marketing. Because it is a subject that is unique to each type of product or service, industry and channel, it would be difficult to create a universally helpful document. The same is true for Manufacturing. There is extensive literature about the basic organization of manufacturing processes. Most specific company problems would not have wide appeal.

During the past fifteen years I have come to greatly admire the work of the Acton Institute for the Study of Religion and Liberty, Grand Rapids, MI. The founder of the Acton Institute, Rev. Robert A. Sirico, has been a tireless, eloquent and effective proponent for the free market system. Father Sirico and his staff spend much of their time and resources training seminarians of all religious faiths about the morality and ethical values of the entrepreneurial vocation. Because of the work of the Acton Institute, I have personally concluded that entrepreneurial capitalism can be a great moral and ethical good in our society. Christians need only read and reflect on the Parable of the Talents (Matthew 25: 14-30) to hear the message about investment and the proper use of the resources available to us. Regardless of your religious persuasion, I believe everyone can see the natural connection between business opportunities and the need to be effective stewards. We are each called upon to use the business resources at our disposal as creatively and productively as possible. Our mission is to increase the value of our holdings in an honest, ethical fashion. Each of us some day must give an accounting of our stewardship. Let us each strive to approach that day by managing the assets entrusted to us as well as we can. To all those who read this book, I hope you are helped by its contents. I would be delighted if some reader said, "This book allowed me to become a more effective business person."

ACKNOWLEDGEMENTS

All of us are products of our personal experiences. Often the most valuable lessons are learned from the toughest situations. People we encounter along the way also shape us. Some encounters are brief but telling. Others are long term and help to form us or change our ideas about life and business. I am certainly no exception to these truths.

Throughout my business life especially, I have been most fortunate to work and live within the sphere of many bright, hard working, thoughtful and courageous business leaders. Some were my superiors, others peers and I include many subordinates from whom I learned a great deal. I had a great boss at IBM...my first job out of college...named Bill Kerr. He taught me more about management than anyone I remember.

The most important person in my entire business life has been William C. Lazier. Bill was my mentor, helped me to understand the dynamics of managing a small business and allowed me to participate in equity ownership of several companies he controlled. I owe most of my business success to Bill Lazier and his persistent confidence in my abilities to handle certain business situations well.

My friend, Jim Collins, the author of "Good to Great" and co-author of "Built to Last," has profoundly influenced my view about how to analyze business problems. Kathy Long Holland, a colleague for 14 years, has been a wonderful sounding board, a constructive critic of my ideas and a great friend. So many have helped me, straightened me out or introduced me to their networks. Included in that group are Arthur Addis, Bill Bain, George Farinsky, Keith Kullberg, Robert Mollet, Tom Reiman, Mike Shadbolt, Chen-Chi Yuan, and others too numerous to name.

My greatest "cheerleaders" during my business career have been Evelyn, my wife of 47 years, and my six children, Eileen, Mary, Leigh Anne, Bing, David and John. I am deeply grateful to all these family members and friends who have made my life so rich and full of wonderful experiences. I am especially grateful to Mary who provided a most helpful edit for this book. Thanks, also, to Ellen Brooks who is responsible for the design of the cover.

I feel blest that all of you have been so helpful and caring to me.

WHAT IT TAKES TO START A BUSINESS

How many of us, while working for a company, have experienced moments of frustration with our situation? Dealing with an unresponsive bureaucracy, an incompetent boss or indifferent co-workers have led us to say, "If I was in charge, things would be different...and better." Perhaps in a quiet moment, a brilliant idea about a revolutionary new product or an unmet consumer need explodes in our mind. With crystal clarity we see how we could execute this great new concept if only we were in control of events. Whether the idea germinates for a long time or suddenly develops, many people exercise their entrepreneurial instinct and begin thinking about starting a business of their own. This intellectual journey may lead to investigating franchise opportunities, considering the purchase of an existing business or actually starting something from scratch. For some anthropological reason, the idea of owning one's own business seems to be unusually strong in the USA. Perhaps it is the long history of entrepreneurial success in this country or the availability of all the needed resources. Whatever the reasons, complex or simple, many people reach a decision in their lives to go off on their own to start or buy a business.

This is a decision that is full of risk. The statistics about failure rates for newly formed businesses are daunting. In spite of this, almost endless waves of enthusiastic and optimistic budding entrepreneurs throw themselves into the steamy cauldron of business. They commit themselves, their fortunes and their reputations to succeeding in these new ventures. Little do they know that the road ahead may be full of potholes, landmines, fear and anxiety, impossible choices and improbable events.

But, we do not mean to discourage. Statistics about business failures are just that...statistics. The crushing defeats happen to the other guys. "I am one

1

of the handful who will exceed in spite of the odds," says the budding entrepreneur. There are success stories reported in the press everyday about fast
growing, highly profitable new companies. Everyone, at the beginning,
believes they will be successful, too. Good luck to them! And we should all be
thankful that there are people who are willing to put everything on the line to
start a new business. A very large part of our thriving economy is based on
small and emerging businesses, the jobs they provide and the contribution
they make to our complex economic systems.

Hundreds, perhaps thousands, of books and articles have been published
about what you need to consider when starting a new business. The purpose
here is to distill the current literature, along with my own personal experience,
into one simple, easy to read document that considers the key things to be
examined in starting up a business. My objective is to provide you with a
checklist of the crucial tasks and decisions to be considered *before* making that
final and irreversible decision to "step off the curb." In broad terms, there are
at least five major topics that must be examined at the front end of the process
to start a business.

- How does this new venture contribute to my life's goals? Have I found
  a business vehicle about which I can be passionate? Do I clearly understand what it takes to be successful?

- Have I thought through the proper form of organization for my venture? Are the tax consequences, risk of liability and ability to finance
  well understood?

- What kind of financial resources will I need to be successful? Where
  will I find these resources? Do I understand the crucial issues of risk
  and control involved?

- How do I deal with the professionals who will inevitably be a part of
  the overall process? Do I understand how to manage the lawyers,
  accountants, venture capitalists, bankers and "angels" so they won't
  wind up managing me?

- Do I have an "exit" strategy? If I have partners or co-investors, is there
  is clear method for people to get out without rancor? Do I understand
  how to deal with colleagues whose individual goals diverge from mine
  and/or the goals of the organization?

The balance of this chapter addresses each of these five points.

How Does This Proposed New Venture Suit Me Personally?

Fools rush in where angels fear to tread. One of the crucial mistakes often made is to fall in love with a deal to start a new company. Remember...the deal will not love you back. According to Marty Marshall, Professor at the Harvard Business School, this is referred to as the "E-I-H Syndrome." The "Entrepreneur in Heat" becomes a panting and irrational being when he or she finds the deal that *must be done* and don't try to confuse me with facts. You think this doesn't happen? It is more the norm than the exception. How does one guard against this syndrome? By stepping back to both ask and answer the following questions in a thoughtful way.

- What do I really want and need out of life? Am I getting *into* something or trying to get *out* of something? Do my style, personality and goals seem to fit this new venture?

- In what specific ways will the new venture contribute to reaching my life's goals?

- Is this a business activity that I can be truly passionate about? Without passion will I be able to deal with the future trials and tribulations faced by many business owners?

- What are the *Key Success Factors* for the new venture? Do I have a good idea of the crucial things that must be done to make the venture successful?

- Do I know how to prioritize the *Key Success Factors*? Will I be able to execute them all at once?

- What are the factors external to the new venture that may determine success? What factors internal to the venture will also be influential on success?

- Do I have a pretty good idea about the appropriate form of organization needed to make the new venture successful? What factors will be most influential on my final decision?

- What type of organizational structure is needed for the general flow of work to be accomplished?

- What are the types, frequency and quality of information that are necessary for the new venture to achieve success?

- What human, technical, facility, equipment and financial resources are likely to be needed for the new venture to be successful?

- What general types of strategic and tactical planning systems will be needed?

- What types of feedback/evaluation systems are required to measure performance?

- What system of rewards and incentives should be adopted to motivate all involved?

- What general management style is most appropriate to the venture?

- How do the answers to the entire set of these questions suit the personality of the Founder and his or her key associates and colleagues in the new venture?

Answering the above questions as thoroughly and objectively as possible will go a long way to keep you from making the classic "E-I-H" mistake. Write down your answers and assessments. That helps you to see how you *really* feel about some of these issues.

What is the Proper Form of Organization for the New Venture?

A lack of care or diligence in answering this question may come back to bite you hard at a later date. While you can assess many of the business and personal considerations, you must get some professional help from a lawyer and accountant before reaching a final decision. This choice will have a crucial effect on taxation, personal liability and your ability to finance the venture. Excluding a franchise contract or buying an existing business, you will probably decide on one of the following five organizational forms. As you will note, each of them have both advantages and disadvantages depending on the situation.

The Sole Proprietorship. This is a basic form of organization and probably the most widely used form for small businesses. The owner/operator and the business are as one. Good examples found in every community are, for example, the residential gardener, the local locksmith, small appliance repairman or auto mechanic among others. If their operations make money, they keep the profits (after paying personal income taxes). If there are losses, they must bear them personally. Other than applying for a local business license or setting up a DBA ("doing business as" name, e.g., A1 Locksmith, John Smith Proprietor) no other formal action is usually required. Federal and state tax returns are filed showing revenue, expenses and profits (if any) from the business. Losses cannot be directly deducted on your personal tax returns but you do have the right to carry them for ward to future years to offset profits under current federal tax laws. The sole proprietor is liable for all his or her business debts; consequently, all other personal assets may also be at risk to satisfy these debts. It is difficult to obtain a bank loan or otherwise raise capital for the sole proprietor. Without substantial personal collateral to offer a bank or other lending institution, the only funds available to the business may be from personal savings, bank credit cards, family and friends. One of the major problems with a sole proprietorship is business continuity and the opportunity to sell the business at some retirement date. In summary: This form is fast, easy, uncomplicated and relatively inexpensive. However, it does not shield the owner from liability, is difficult to finance and has little ability to extend business continuity after the founder is gone.

General or Limited Partnership. This structure is created by agreement between the partners. The agreement definitely should be reduced to writing. The agreement spells out each partner's ownership interest in the partnership, how much each partner is investing in the venture, the division of work, how long the partnership is to last, what happens in the event of death of a partner and how the agreement can be terminated. Attempting to structure an agreement that covers all the potential situations the partners may face in the future may result in a very complicated document. Regarding taxes, each partner is usually (not always) given credit for a proportionate share of the partnership's profit or loss and files his or her own tax returns. In a General Partnership all partners assume joint and several responsibilities for all liabilities. In other words, each partner is theoretically responsible for *all the liabilities* of the partnership, not just his or her pro rata share. In a Limited Partnership, the General Partner(s) assume joint and several liability for all the partnership's liabilities but the Limited Partners are only liable up to their pro rata share of the equity invested. By their very nature, partnerships are difficult to make work. Two or more people may start out in a venture with complete unity of purpose and shared values. However, time sometimes causes partners to diverge in their goals, objectives and values. It is critical for equal partners to have a mechanism in place to settle disputes which are sure to come up over time. Like the Sole Proprietorship, financing a partnership's needs can be difficult with traditional lenders. Solid collateral and personal guarantees are almost always required for debt financing. It is also somewhat difficult for a small partnership to provide business continuity. Dealing with the death of a partner may also cause financial and continuity problems. In summary: The partnership has its place especially for professional ventures like law, accounting or medical associations and certain real estate ventures. However, the growth of the Limited Liability Corporation or Partnership may be making the concept of the general partnership passé.

The "C" (Regular) Corporation. Under the law, a corporation is considered as a distinct entity like a person. The fundamental advantage of the corporate form is that individual shareholders may be sheltered from liability. In virtually every case, an individual investor's liability is limited to the amount he or she has invested in the company. Creditors are normally limited to corporate assets when seeking to collect money owed. This limitation on liability *may* not apply to a company owned by one or two people when individual and corporate assets are co-mingled. In that case, a creditor may attempt to "pierce the corporate veil" by claiming the corporation is a sham merely to improperly shelter the owners of the company from liability. A corporation may be easier to finance because of its ability to issue stock. The C Corporation is more complicated regarding set-up, reporting requirements and the need for professional advice and services. To get started, you must file Articles of Incorporation, create a set of by-laws and satisfy other state requirements depending on which state will be the legal home for the corporation. Different states have more or less favorable laws for corporations set up in their jurisdictions. For example, you may have a corporation set up in one state but with all its operations located in another state. A corporation may be subject to extensive regulatory scrutiny and must maintain corporate reports and activities as required by the state authorities. Tax returns are often more complicated. Depending on the current political climate, corporate tax rates on income may be more, or less, than on individuals. Currently dividends paid to shareholders are taxable to the individual recipients but are not tax deductible to the corporation. Taxation often extends to both the corporation and the shareholder. This may be especially crucial if there is a sale of the corporation stock or assets at a future date. There is no limit to the number of shareholders in a C Corporation. The corporation also provides the perfect vehicle for business continuity since there is often a broad base of shareholders and management can be hired to run the company by the Board of Directors. In a closely held corporation, shareholders often have an agreement which allows them to dispose of their shares. In a public company, shares are often traded in public meaning there is a ready market to dispose of or acquire shares in the company. In summary: The corporation has the fundamental advantage of shielding individual shareholders from liability. The corporation will normally have an easier time raising money because it can issue shares in exchange for equity investments. The corporation also can provide excellent continuity for the venture. On the other hand, the corporation is more complicated to set up, is subject to regulatory scrutiny and reporting, and can create some tax disadvantages for both the company and individual shareholders. The C Corporation may be an excellent organizational form for the venture that expects to grow into a very large operation in the future. It may not be the best form for a small, privately held firm.

The Subchapter "S" Corporation. Like the C Corporation, the S Corporation is a distinct legal entity that provides the shareholders with limited liability. The S Corporation also offers potential tax advantages. S Corporations elect to have their profits taxed as if their shareholders were partners or sole proprietors. Ordinary income and loss is passed through to the individual shareholders and reported on their personal income tax returns. The tax rates for individuals may be lower than the corporate rate. The initial set-up of the S Corporation is similar to that of a C Corporation. Corporate governance, regulatory scrutiny and required reporting requirements will be similar to C Corporations in most jurisdictions. The S Corporation does have some specific restrictions. For example, the number of shareholders is limited to 35 (primarily individuals, estates and certain trusts and may not currently include foreign nationals). To be eligible for S Corporation status, there can only be one class of stock outstanding although voting rights may differ. The S Corporation is often an excellent corporate form for the small business. The company can probably raise working capital financing but it may not be able to offer shares to investors. The S Corporation also can avoid the double taxation faced by the C Corporation if the company and/or the assets are sold at a future time. In summary: The S Corporation is will suited to the small business who wishes to shield its shareholders from liability. Depending on tax rates, profits as reported by shareholders on their tax returns may be less than corporate rates paid by C Corporations. The S Corporation can probably borrow to satisfy working capital needs but is restricted by the number of shareholders from raising equity capital from a large base of shareholders.

Limited Liability Corporation (LLC) and Limited Liability Partnership (LLP). These are relatively new forms of corporate organization. Be sure to check with your governing authority to make sure they have been approved for use in your own state. The LLC provides the shareholders with the same limited liability of a C or S Corporation but it has the tax status and flexibility of a partnership. Getting the LLC set up will be similar to a C or S Corporation. Taxation is reported on shareholders' personal tax returns rather than on a corporate return. There are negative aspects of raising capital since the organization is viewed as a partnership. There are also questions about succession planning so that corporate continuity can be maintained. The LLP is generally replacing the General Partnership as a organizational form for attorneys, accountants and medical practices.

The information provided above about each of these types of corporate form is considered to be accurate at the time it was written. However, this is an evolving area of business and tax law. It would be a serious mistake if you did not contact your legal and tax advisors prior to making a decision about what form is appropriate for your new venture. With some of the key information in hand, we hope that you will be able to work more closely with your professional advisors in making the proper choices that will work best for you.

How Do I Determine, Find and Secure the Financial Resources Needed for Success?

There are many ways to finance the operations of a new business venture. Entrepreneurs seeking funding will often turn first to their own personal savings. If those funds are insufficient approaches may be made to family and friends hoping they might lend or invest. The next source of funding comes from *secured* sources of capital including aggressive banks, factors, accounts receivable finance companies, general commercial credit firms, leasing companies, real estate lenders and government funding programs. There are also *unsecured* sources of funding such as venture capital firms or corporate strategic alliance partners. Finally, there is *adventure* capital provided by informal investors (called "angels") who are often comprised of professionals like doctors, dentists, lawyers and accountants, senior business executives or other entrepreneurs. It is unlikely that a small startup will attract the interest of unsecured or adventure capital. That does not mean you shouldn't investigate whether or not your venture might be interesting to these sources of capital. A basic Internet search will provide you with abundant contact information on many of these sources. Also, please refer to Chapter 3 of this book, "Convincing a Bank to Loan You Money." This information provides you with a guide to borrowing from a commercial bank.

Finding financing sources may, or may not, be easy. Before making contact with these potential sources you must first determine how much financing you are going to need. This means you must create a detailed written business plan for your new venture. This document is a lot more than just a set of financial projections showing revenue, expenses, the build up of assets and liabilities and the cash requirements of the business over some fixed period of time. Of primary importance is a crystal clear explanation of your proposed product or service, the marketing strategy to be employed and the people and organization that will execute the plan. You must do a thorough job on your business plan to attract the interest of some financing sources. As a guide to developing this plan, ask yourself the following questions:

- Does the business have a realistic chance to grow into a successful company? Why do you think so?

- Have you thoroughly researched the market to insure that there is a need for your product or service at a price that will be profitable for you? Who are your major competitors?

- Have you selected co-founders and colleagues with appropriate credentials, experience and enthusiasm for your new venture? Will they work well together?

- Do you understand that investors only risk their money when they see a reasonable chance for an adequate return on their investment? Can you show them how that will happen?

- Do you have the unqualified support of your family and friends? Do you understand the serious personal and financial commitment associated with starting a new business?

Develop thorough and honest answers to these questions. It will help you to understand the risks and rewards of starting your own business and to appreciate the difficult tasks lying ahead. To prepare yourself for this new venture, speak with other entrepreneurs, your accountant, your attorney and business people you trust and admire. All of these people can offer you important words of wisdom about what to expect and how to get your venture launched.

Writing a thorough and compelling business plan is hard work. Once again, you will find that the Internet is your friend when you investigate how others have created their business plans. Don't make the mistake of using a "cookie cutter" approach to your written plan that is full of "boiler plate" content adding only empty words. Make sure what you write is credible, well thought out, well researched and focused on *your* venture. Investors are not impressed by the size of the business plan, just the content. Start out by creating a detailed outline of all the topics to be covered. Also, put together the following information before you actually begin the job of producing the plan.

- Resumes of you, your co-founders and key associates.

- Historical statistics and credible projections about the market you will be addressing.

- Relevant magazine, newspaper and internet information about your industry.

- Names of probable competitors and information about them.

- Names of key potential customers and/or classes of customers you will approach.

- Laws, regulations and government actions that could affect the business.

- Potential patent, copyright or trademark information that is relevant.

- Material and labor cost data and availability.

The single most important part of your business plan is the Executive Summary. Often just one or two pages, this highlights important details about the opportunity, the market, products, the key people and why the venture is expected to succeed. Typical investors routinely receive a large volume of unsolicited business plans. They will often glance at the Executive Summary to see if there is a story that interests them. Seldom will investors read your entire plan at the first sitting. If you write a credible and compelling Executive Summary, there is a good chance the investor will pick the document up and begin reading more about what you plan to do. On the other hand, a weak Executive Summary will probably doom even the most promising venture. Remember this important fact: *The Executive Summary is what will get the investor to read further or call you for additional information.* It is clearly the most crucial part of your business plan.

What about the rest of the plan? What information should be included? After looking at hundreds of business plans, the following generalized outline distills the key components included in most plans. No two plans will ever be exactly alike.

- The Executive Summary (discussed above).

- General background information about the market, the products, the industry.

- Detailed review of the marketplace including segmentation.

- The product or service—what it does, its uniqueness, its place in the market.

- The marketing plan including channel selection, barriers to entry and strategic assumptions.

- A detailed review of competition.

- Our proprietary position; how we will differentiate ourselves.

- A production plan; strategy related to being a low cost producer, if appropriate.

- Explain the facilities and capital equipment needed to execute the production plan.

- Human resources required; availability of skills required to be successful.

- Organization plan; internal control metrics required; feedback mechanisms.

- Financial projections.

  - Detailed assumptions underlying the projections.

  - Income statements; 1 year by month; 2 years by quarter; 2 years annual.

  - Balance sheets; 1 year by month; 2 years by quarter; 2 years annual.

  - Sources and uses of cash for five years as above.

- Proposed financing transaction.

- The capital structure, the timing of seeking liquidity, the exit strategy.

- Risk factors.

- Addendums: Industry information, magazine articles, other validated research data.

After completing a draft business plan, compare it to the following check list for completeness.

- Is the definition of the proposed business clear?

- Are all strategy explanations complete?

- Is the information presented on the founders and key associates sufficient?

- Is the information about the market complete and compelling? (This is absolutely crucial).

- Is the staffing proposal and organization plan sensible?

- Are the action plans and priorities regarding the first year, in particular, very specific?

- Are the financing plans clear?

- Is there adequate detailed information for further analysis?

- Is the plan well written?

- Can one make an objective evaluation based on the facts presented?

Show your draft to as many people as possible. You are not looking for cheerleaders; you want people to review the plan critically and point out what they think may be weaknesses or "holes." As a final check, find a good general proofreader and editor to read the plan. Your document must be professional, free of misspellings, poor grammar and easy to read.

A key byproduct of producing a business plan is that you now have an indication of how much financing you will need (at least during the five years of the plan). At this stage, you have done two things that were required. You have probably identified a universe of financing sources that may have some interest in your opportunity. You have also determined, in general, how much financing you will require. Now comes the hard part—securing the financing needed. There is no magic to this task. If your business plan was a product, how would you market it? You would put together a marketing plan, researching the people that might be most interested in buying the product. You would then prioritize these people and call on the best and most likely prospects first. It is exactly the same for your business plan. Figure out who might be most interested in your plan. Figure out a way to get their attention and call on them. Have a presentation prepared. Learn from prospects' questions that you find hard to answer. Refine your presentation. Re-work your plan. Keep iterating and working until someone finally says, "I like what you have presented. Let's talk some more about this situation."

Most entrepreneurs are looking for the "silver bullet" that opens doors and attracts money quickly and effortlessly. It doesn't work that way. There are hundreds of entrepreneurs and business plans competing for the attention of the investor group that can make dreams reality. To emerge victorious in this fiercely competitive environment, you must be one of the smarter, harder working and more tenacious individuals. If you really believe in your business plan and yourself, you will do what it takes to make your idea happen. Good luck!

How to Deal with the Professionals.

To the ordinary layman it can be intimidating to deal with someone whose business card identifies him or her as "Attorney at Law" or "Certified Public Accountant." No matter what your educational background or life experience may be, many people may feel that the attorney or CPA has special skills, especially related to complicated business transactions, providing them with an advantage. This wariness we may have is further emphasized to us by the nervous jokes told about the professions: "Lawyers—99% of them give the rest a bad name," and hundreds more ad nauseam. In fact, anyone contemplating launching a new business venture had better understand the vital role legal and accounting professionals will play in your eventual success. Along the way, you may also encounter investment bankers, merchant bankers, financing consultants, commercial bankers, loan brokers, intermediaries and others who exist in the middle of this world of finance. In every case, these professionals have some specific in-depth knowledge about a portion of funding activity that may be greater than the entrepreneur seeking the money. Those seeking funding have two choices. You can decide to be cowed by these folks and allow them to set the terms upon which you will finance your venture. Or, you can resolve to respect their knowledge and ability to help you but insist that you will have a co-equal role with them in determining the conditions of the funding. In other words, you can let the professionals manage you or you can decide to manage them.

Merely saying you will manage this activity doesn't mean it's going to unfold exactly the way you want it. It does mean that the entrepreneur will take an aggressive proactive role in each step along the financing journey. He or she does that by asking questions until satisfied he or she understands the alternatives available and insisting that mutually beneficial agendas for the process are established in advance of action. The entrepreneur who does his or her homework, making himself or herself knowledgeable about the financing process, and requires his or her input to be an important part of the final solution has a much better chance of being adequately funded on terms that he or she can live with down the line.

If you are seeking secured financing from a commercial bank, commercial credit company or similar source, there are fairly standard conditions surrounding each loan and many formulae about how much collateral is required to secure the loan. Control issues are not quite as prevalent with secured financing but most loans do contain many performance covenants that may limit your operational control. When you are looking for unsecured equity financing from those generally referred to as Venture Capitalists, control aspects may be much more stringent. For example, securing equity capital may require that you give up a very large portion of your corporation. You may be required to offer seats on your Board of Directors to those who supply the funding. There may also be performance benchmarks and investment criteria you must meet in order to receive additional funding. These control provisions are not necessarily bad but you must be aware they will be placed on the table during negotiations for the funding. "Angel" investors may not be as demanding as the traditional Venture Capitalists.

Retaining an attorney and accountant that you trust and have confidence in will be a vital step on your path to success. How do you find them? Talk to other business people, members of your service club and others in the community for references. Go and visit them armed with the following questions.

- How long have you been in practice? Are you a sole practitioner or do you have associates? Will I be working with you directly or will you be handing me off to a more junior member of the firm?

- Do you have clients in my industry? If "yes," do you see any conflict because of confidential information? If "no," do you understand the dynamics of my business venture well enough to give me good advice?

- Does your practice specialize in any aspect of the law?

- How busy is your practice? I don't want to be ignored or put off when I call for help or advice. Can you assure me that I will receive adequate attention from your firm when I seek assistance?

- Why should I engage you instead of another firm? How will my dealings with you assist me in making my firm more efficient and my life easier?

- What are your professional rates? For yourself? For your associates?

- I will insist on an itemized monthly bill. Will that be any problem for you to provide? How will you bill me for copies, messenger delivery and other ancillary services?

And, the following additional questions should be asked of the CPA or accounting firm.

- To what extent are you willing and/or able to provide advice beyond just completing financial statements and tax returns? Do you have resources inside/outside your firm you can call upon to help me with such things as computer problems, networks, installations, etc?

- What routine accounting functions do you handle, if any? For example, will your staff keep the depreciation schedules or fixed asset ledger up to date if we ask you to do this for us? Upon request, will you provide oversight when we produce interim financial statement or will you just be involved at year end?

- Given what you know about our business records and tax returns, can you provide an estimate of what your fees might be on a yearly basis? What things would make a material change in this estimate? Will your services provide us with a compiled, reviewed or audited financial statements? What increase in fees would you require for reviewed or audited financial statements?

- We are not trained accountants. Do you and your staff have the patience to work effectively with non-professional personnel and still produce accurate, reliable and timely financial information? Don't say "yes" unless you mean it.

No matter how good a businessperson you may be or what a super negotiator you are, you will require the assistance of a competent attorney for every transaction you do. You need legal expertise to make sure the business deal, building lease, vendor contract, etc., is finalized in a proper legal document protecting everyone's rights and spelling out legal obligations for all parties. The same may be said for the accounting professional whose services are needed to insure your financial reporting and tax returns are accurate, honest and properly constructed. In summary, do not simply defer to these important professionals but create a climate where they are considered as invaluable partners in important areas of your business operations.

What is the Exit Strategy for You, Your Colleagues and Your Investors?

For a complete discussion of this subject please refer to the chapter in this book, "The Next Step; Planning a Succession/Harvest/Exit Strategy."

Just about the last thing one thinks about when starting a new venture is, "How am I going to get out of this?" At the beginning of a task like starting a business, the mind and body are consumed in trying to accomplish all the work required to get the company up and running. How can a person possibly think about the events down the road when it may be time to leave this venture? It is easy to understand the human focus on the here and now. Events along the way will determine what the future holds. I will worry about the future in the future. In the meantime, I need to get this business underway.

Just because you're too busy right now to think about exit strategies does not mean they are not crucially important. Not only for you but also for your co-founders and investors the issue of eventual exit looms large right from the beginning. While certain aspects of exit strategy may be finally decided and implemented at a future date, several important questions must be addressed at the very beginning of the venture.

- For you personally, why are you *really* doing this? Early on in this chapter we suggested you ask yourself, "How does this new venture add to my life's goals and objectives?" It can be assumed that part of your future involves the accumulation of some material wealth. How much wealth do you wish to acquire? Will this company be the vehicle for reaching this part of your life's objectives? If you haven't thought about these questions or formulated general answers (as a minimum) you may be lacking an important focus in your life. To say, "I'll just work hard for a few years and see how things turn out," is an inadequate answer to a very important question.

- There may be co-founders or key associates who will share in the ownership of the new company. No doubt you will all start out perfectly unified with totally compatible ideas about how the business should develop. Time has a way of changing ideas and priorities for people. In the life of most ventures, there is a divergence of objectives between the people who initially founded the firm. Concepts that created total agreement suddenly are affected by elements of disunity. People once close emotionally, intellectually and philosophically become distant and remote. While this doesn't always happen, it *can* happen. If and when it does, there can be a problem that tears at the fabric of the company. To prevent any future rifts, it is vital to create an initial agreement between shareholders and major stakeholders detailing how exit from the firm is to be handled. If this is decided and memorialized in an agreement early on, people who no longer share the values or ambitions of the majority can leave the firm on a basis that is economically fair and causes no rancor. In this matter, exit planning is most important to the future potential health and value of the firm.

- If venture capital is involved, the funding providers want to clearly understand how their money will be returned and when. For some firms, this may be an Initial Public Offering (IPO) when stock is offered to the general public and the venture investors have an opportunity to redeem their equity in the company. In other cases, the venture investors will be able to cash out when the company is sold or merged. In any event, providers of venture capital are looking for near certainty about when and how they will be able to get out. This means that the founders must carefully consider a strategy to satisfy the equity investors from the very formation of the business.

No matter how you rationalize, you cannot avoid developing exit strategies from the very beginning of the firm. What happens when you don't? You have little way of gauging how you are reaching your personal goals. Your co-founders and colleagues may become disenchanted with the business...or you...and want a way out. With no exit strategy in place this can be an emotionally draining and expensive experience. Finally, if you have attracted venture capital your investors will press you for a firm commitment about how and when they will be able to redeem their investment in the firm. A well-thought out and realistic exit strategy must be part of the initial planning for any new venture.

Many people have started up new businesses without following the advice provided here. Some, to be sure, have succeeded in spite of a failure to plan. Starting the company, overcoming the many obstacles encountered along the way, finally reaching "lift off" and then achieving ultimate success is hard enough for anyone. You can make this task somewhat easier by following the simple suggestions offered above.

GET CREATIVE ABOUT YOUR CORPORATE GOVERNANCE

Virtually every state in the United States requires some form of Board of Directors for corporations registered in their jurisdiction. For many small, privately held companies, the Board is a formality that was set up when the corporation was established. As time goes on, the corporate attorney nags the business owner to at least hold an annual Board meeting and submit a set of minutes so that corporate records will be up to date. Often, the Board of a small company consists of: (1) a husband and wife owner team; (2) unrelated partners in the venture; (3) the owner and his attorney and accountant; (4) some other group of related parties and/or family members. Seldom does one find a small company Board composed of objective, detached outsiders. Boards of Directors, therefore, seldom provide much guidance, direction and support to the operating management of the smaller corporation. Boards are usually considered a legally required nuisance. Even though they may be viewed as a legal necessity, membership on Boards of Directors can carry onerous potential for liability. This is true even in small, privately-held companies especially if there is a group of shareholders. For these reasons plus a desire for privacy, a simple aversion to scrutiny, fear of losing control of the corporation and inertia, most entrepreneurial business owners have not formed an active Board of Directors.

This doesn't mean they don't need outside counsel. One of the greatest problems for owners of small companies is isolation. As the saying goes, "It's lonely at the top." Who does the business owner turn to when faced with a difficult, perplexing problem? A spouse may be interested and sympathetic but lacks background or insight. Certain matters cannot be shared with key employees. Advice on business issues from an attorney, accountant or other fiduciary may be conflicted. Often the business owner will lack expertise or experience in a certain area. It would be most helpful to have an expert resource to call upon for advice and guidance. Myopia can be a serious problem when related to business decisions. What are the alternative courses of action for a particular situation? Sometimes this can be very hard for a business owner to see by himself or herself. The owner frequently needs a detached, objective outside view of the situation. At other times it would be helpful to have an advocate to employees, family or investors. The owner needs a sounding board for potential decisions, new ideas and to work through impending crises. In short, virtually every small business owner needs some type of "kitchen cabinet" to provide advice, counsel, perspective, objectivity and frequent "reality checks" in the work-a-day world of commerce.

A solution for this problem is to form an Advisory Committee. This is in addition to, not in place of, the corporation's Board of Directors. There is a need for both groups because they perform different functions. Most significantly, a Board of Directors represents *all* shareholders in a corporation. It is also a more permanent body with quite specific duties and obligations. There is a large body of written material about Boards of Directors and the author encourages you to research and find what you require. By contrast, the purpose of this chapter is to outline what an Advisory Committee is, what it does, where you find the advisors and how to structure and effectively use the Committee.

Creating as active Advisory Committee can offer many substantial benefits to almost any entrepreneurial company.

> *Perspective and Experience.* First and foremost, the breadth and depth of experiences that outside Advisors may bring to the table can be extremely valuable. The business owner may lack specific skill in marketing, finance, human relations, etc. Having an Advisor with a complementary background can be most useful especially when important decisions are being considered.

> *Vision and Insight.* If an Advisor is, or has been, an entrepreneur or CEO, he or she can be uniquely able to provide the advice that an insider will not be able to offer to the business owner.

> *Business Control.* Advisors can help provide a framework of control and discipline that may be lacking in some small business environments. Showing the business owner how to plan, budget and monitor results can

make a significant contribution to improving the operations of a company.

Role Clarification. Advisors can be most useful in sorting out possible different interests of key management, family members and shareholders. Advisors can also assist the owner by sometimes acting as advocates to the various constituencies of the company, both internal and external.

Continuity and Succession. Advisors can be helpful in dealing with the issue of succession planning in a company. Most small companies do not address this matter forthrightly. Advisors can be especially useful in dealing with generational transition issues in family-owned businesses.

Sounding Board. Advisors can give the owner emotional support and an objective perspective needed when especially difficult business decisions are being considered. This is most helpful when dealing with matters of health, family, termination of key employees and major financial events.

Objectivity. Advisors are able to provide the owner with objective alternatives from a variety of different business cultures. A qualified, trusted outside Advisor will feel free to tell the business owner the truth, no matter how rough that may be.

Compensation and Performance Review. Advisors give the owner someone to consult with regarding compensation and performance reviews of key employees. In fact, the owner may benefit by asking the Advisors to frankly review his or her own performance and compensation package.

Long-Term Strategic Planning. This area often suffers in smaller businesses because of the press of day-to-day activities. The frequent cry is, "We never have time to do planning." Advisors can help the owner create a climate and recognition of the need for long-term planning. Advisors, while discussing and reviewing the owner's long-range strategies, are uniquely free of internal prejudice with this issue.

Complementary Skills. Properly selected Advisors should fill the "skill gaps" with the organization by sharing their complementary talents and experiences with the owner.

Credibility. Particularly when the company is small, the presence of experienced businesspersons on the Advisory Committee lends an air of credibility that can be important to potential customers, vendors, lenders and other outsiders. It often shows that the company is serious about creating a strong, growing business.

Networking. Advisors can be invaluable in providing introductions to key individuals and institutions. This can be effective in recruiting, developing strategic alliances, financing the company and finding new customers and clients.

This list above describes only some of the ways in which an Advisory Committee may benefit a small or emerging company and its owners.

OK, this may sound like a good idea so far. But where and how does one find the right people to serve as Advisors to a company? Start by seeking recommendations from the company lawyer, accountant, banker and other key people that interact with the firm. Please note that it is *definitely not* suggested that people with a fiduciary relationship be asked to serve on an Advisory Committee. The business owner needs to have his or her decisions examined competently in the harsh light of business reality. A risk-taking peer, someone who is not indebted to the company in any way best does this. The business owner needs Advisors from *outside* the business or family and who are not professional service providers to the firm. For a secondary source of referrals, the owner should consult with business acquaintances, members of his or her service clubs and to other CEO's in the community. To be effective in this search, the principal must have a pretty good idea of the skills and qualifications that are being sought in potential Advisors. Consider the following characteristics.

Trust and Chemistry. Nothing works unless there is a high degree of mutual trust and personal chemistry between the Advisor and owner. The Advisor will hear lots of private and confidential things. He or she must be expected to act like the owner's priest, rabbi or minister in respecting confidentiality.

Diversity. Look for Advisors who offer diverse, complementary skills. Get one who is strong in marketing, another in finance, yet another in distribution, etc. Don't try to clone yourself.

Integrity. Absolute honesty, fair dealing, courage to disagree and stand up for his or her beliefs—this is what is needed in an Advisor. The owner wants someone who will always tell the truth no matter how harsh that may be.

Mesa County Libraries
970-243-4442
mesacountylibraries.org

Thank you for checking out the
following items:

Item Title	Due Date
Le cerf-volant 1090008123665	**12-20-15**
Roma 1090007735738	**12-20-15**
Impardonnables 1090010003773	**12-20-15**
White fire / Douglas 1090010176220	**01-03-16**

Already Busy. Exceptional Advisors are often very busy already. They may be serving on other Advisory Committees and Boards of Directors. Those people should be sought out. There is one exception to this advice. Potential Advisors who are directly involved in start-ups or turnaround situations are probably *too busy* to be of assistance to another company.

A Special Kind of Friend. An Advisor should be a friend, but not in a social sense. The real friend is one who wants the best for you and will bluntly tell you if you're getting off the track. A real friend will carefully prepare for each Advisory Committee meeting and will take the job of being an Advisor very seriously.

Finding good Advisors to serve isn't an easy job. However, if well done, it is a task that can pay handsome rewards for the business owner and his or her company.

How does an Advisory Committee work, exactly? What are the administrative details that you need to know about?

Meetings. Meetings should be scheduled at least quarterly. You may wish to have more frequent meetings (perhaps monthly) initially to bring all Advisors "up to speed" with your business and the important issues you are facing.

Agendas. At least one week prior to every meeting, you should prepare a detailed agenda and forward it along with your current financial information to each Advisor. The agenda should be very specific about topics to be addressed. This information, sent with the minimum one-week leadtime, will permit the Advisors to come to the meeting prepared.

Meeting Minutes. During the initial meeting, a recording secretary should be appointed so that detailed minutes are produced. The minutes should be working notes rather than formal minutes produced in a Board of Directors meeting. The purpose of these notes is to memorialize the proceedings, especially the action items that have been agreed upon.

Length of Meetings. Because you are busy running your business and the Advisors have plenty on their plates, too, total meeting time should not exceed three hours. Two hours is better.

Compensation for Advisors. No one serves as an Advisory Committee member to get rich. However, it is important to compensate your Advisors for their time commitment. They are entitled to typical professional rates for their service. Therefore, fees of $300-$500 per meeting per Advisor are appropriate. Just as with Boards of Directors, it is usual and customary to present the fees to the Advisors at the meeting.

Number of Advisors. There are no hard and fast rules about the number of Advisors you should engage. However, experience indicates that three outside Advisors represents the optimum number. This will provide the meetings with enough synergy and positive dynamics to make the session most effective. A larger number of Advisors can tend to bog down meetings too much.

Managing the Committee. Remember, the Advisors chosen will probably have strong egos because of what they have accomplished in their lives. You're going to have to do a good job of managing their egos effectively. Don't let your meetings get off track or away from the published agenda.

Position Descriptions. As part of your initial organization of your Advisory Committee you may wish to create some position descriptions for an Advisor. This may help them, and you, judge how well they are performing their role on your Committee.

Standard of Performance. You may also produce a Standard of Performance for the Advisory Committee so that the group can judge how effectively it is performing.

Information Provided to Advisors. You should provide your Advisors with three types of information: that which is permanent, annually updated and monthly. Permanent information should be such things as:

- The corporate statement of core values, purpose and mission,
- Resumes on all key members of management,
- Resumes on the Advisors themselves.

Information to be updated annually might include:

- The corporate organization chart,
- A complete list of key managers, directors and advisors,
- A list of key contractual obligations, i.e., union contracts, leases, etc.,

- Employment agreements or agreements with customers and vendors,

- A list of the company's top 20 customers and 3 major competitors,

- Next year's budget—Income Statement, Balance Sheet and Cash Flow.

Monthly, your Advisors should receive:

- A complete set of financial reports,

- Major changes in personnel, customers or distribution policies,

- Notes about pending litigation,

- A list of possible Negative Occurrences happening in the business.

Three major events occur around each Advisory Committee meeting. First, the business owner and the company's key managers must *prepare in advance* for the meeting by putting together a detailed agenda, updated financial information and other details about the company's condition. That in itself is worthwhile since it forces the company's management to stop periodically and take stock of where they are and where they think they are headed. Second, the meeting itself forces the business owner to stand up in front of his or her Advisors to *explain and defend* his or her recent decisions and plans for the near term future. Objective, candid Advisors may not agree with the owner and voice their disagreement forcefully. This is worthwhile since it requires the owner to carefully think through the plans and be prepared to defend his or her actions to the Advisors. Third, each Advisory Committee meeting will probably conclude with the Advisors outlining *a list of "marching orders"* for the owner—things the Advisors would like to see accomplished prior to the next meeting. These three events, occurring about every 60 working days, can really help to shape the company, keep the owner and key managers focused and provide a framework for a more successful company going forward.

One word of caution. It is wise to create a proper documentation about the duties of an Advisory Committee. The outside world must understand that the company's Advisory Committee is *not* the Board of Directors. You should be careful not to put your advisors at any legal risk. This can be done by keeping good records about what the Advisory Committee and its members do and don't do regarding governance of the business.

Advisory Committees can be a wonderful aid for the owner of a small or emerging business. What you get out of having an Advisory Committee will be in relation to what you, as a business owner, put into it. It is a truism that the best Advisory Committees are found in the best-managed companies. Are you willing to try?

CONVINCING A BANK TO
LOAN YOU MONEY

Maybe you're independently wealthy. Perhaps your Father left you the Hope Diamond. Most small business owners aren't so lucky. When you look for ways to finance your company, you'll find there are three sources of funds—capital you invest out of your own savings, trade credit from suppliers and loans from family, friends, banks and other lenders. The first two may not be adequate, so sometime during the life of your business you will probably approach a bank in search of funds. This process seems shrouded in mystery for the business owner. Should I go to a big regional bank or a local independent? What does the bank look for? How can I figure out—in advance—if I have a chance of borrowing any money? If I do qualify, how much can I expect to borrow? These questions fill the mind of the owner with apprehension as he or she gets ready to visit the bank. Our purpose is to help you understand whether or not the bank will provide a loan, how much can be borrowed and under what conditions and terms. This is not a commercial banking textbook. A thorough reading of this chapter will give you a "feel" for what to expect when approaching a banker for a loan.

A potential borrower must understand that the banking industry has changed in the past 20-25 years. In days past, the banker was on the same pedestal with the doctor, lawyer or minister. He or she was a pillar of the community, the wise financial advisor who loaned his or her bank's money based on his or her view of the character of the borrower. Now, banking is considered as another, albeit important, element of our complex economic system. Today's banker is usually a well-trained financial expert. While he or she may enjoy the respect of peers and customers, the typical banker does not command the same position in society that was once held. Commercial banking makes an important contribution to our market system but the transaction of loaning money is now much more complicated and objective in nature.

What does a banker look for in financing a business? What criteria does the bank use to decide whether or not money will be loaned? Fundamentally, every potential borrower must come with four basic attributes in order to be considered for a loan.

- Good *character*.

- Adequate *collateral*.

- An exemplary *credit history*.

- 2-3 years of *profitable operations*.

In addition, expect to be asked to personally guarantee any loan made to your business. This is virtually an ironclad provision of most bank loans to smaller businesses. If you pass muster on these basic issues, each bank will review your loan request from a slightly different perspective. The following items represent a list of the issues that most banks will consider in evaluating your credit worthiness.

Business Life Cycle. In broad terms, businesses can be described as start-ups, growing or mature. Banks want to know where your business is on the life cycle curve. Start-ups will generally have a hard time attracting bank financing. The bankers are nervous about the lack of operating history and often will deem start-ups too risky a place to invest their customers' demand deposits. Banks do best in assisting companies that are on the growth part of the curve. Mature businesses may attract bank financing if they have a profitable operating history unless they are perceived to be in decline.

What Does the Business Do? This sounds simple enough but it is vitally important to the bank. Can you explain, in clear terms, what business you are actually in, who are your customers, what they specifically buy from you—and why? How does your business work, exactly? The banker wants to know if this is really a viable business. This can be tested with a variety of questions, for example, are the owners paying themselves a salary that provides a reasonable living? Bankers know that some business ventures are inherently more risky than others and will avoid lending money to them. For example, retail businesses are often unstable, restaurants can be volatile and apparel companies with their fashion inventory risks are usually avoided. If your business is considered "risky," it will be more difficult to obtain bank financing.

What Is the Company's Market Position? If there are two grocery stores in a 400-person town, one is probably doing better than the other. So it goes for all business enterprise. What share of the overall market does your company have? Why do customers buy from you instead of your competitors? Conversely, why do you lose business to competitors? What are your opportunities to increase your market share? What threats exist that might cause you to lose market share? Bankers will be most interested in answers to these questions. Banks are more inclined to loan money to companies with a strong or growing market position compared to one whose share is shrinking or in jeopardy.

What is The "Operating Cycle" Of the Business? This is a *crucial* consideration for banks. The Operating Cycle means the time taken by *all the events between a customer order until cash from an invoice is collected and deposited in the bank.* For a manufacturer there may be a selling effort resulting in a customer placing a purchase order. Next comes the acquisition of materials needed to produce the products. Time is then required to manufacture the goods. The completed material is shipped to the customer. An invoice is rendered. Some time passes until the customer pays the bill and funds are deposited in the bank. This sequence of events (that will vary for every business) is referred to as the "operating cycle." It can be further complicated by seasonal factors (Christmas tree farms, fireworks producers, ski equipment manufacturers, etc.). The banker will be most eager to understand precisely how long it takes and the amount of money that may be required to complete the cycle. Important considerations will include credit terms given to customers, the company's ability to collect its accounts receivable promptly and how much of the material and services needed can be financed by accounts payable.

What Does the Future Hold? A buggy whip manufacturer in 1900 may have been very profitable, held a significant market share, tightly controlled its operating cycle…but been a poor credit risk. The same story could be told about black and white TV producers in the 1950's, eight track tape manufacturers in the 1970's or rotary dial telephone makers in the 1980's. The banker wants to know that you have a reasonably bright future for your business. After all, he or she is counting on you to pay him back in the future what he or she has loaned you today. The small business owner must demonstrate to a potential lender that the prospects for continued business, while not guaranteed, look promising.

How Is the Business Organized? The banker does not expect every business to have a depth chart like the San Francisco 49er's, but he or she wants to deal with more than a "one person band." Is a team of people in place to manage the various aspects of the business? What are the backgrounds and qualifications of the key personnel? Are the skill sets in place to handle the contingencies a small business can and does face? Is there a plan for the future to add the necessary people as growth warrants? Are these people readily available? The well-staffed small business is *always* a better credit risk from the banker's prospective.

Product and Customer Diversification. Few things make a banker more nervous than a one-product or one-customer company. Many small businesses start out with just one product or service and initially may have very few customers. Diversification in both these areas should be a high priority. Bankers will be concerned when they see a limited product or service offering. This is a recipe for a competitor to devastate a company overnight. The same concept applies to having only a few customers. Many bankers will shy away from your business if one customer represents as much as 10% of a company's total sales. In theory, you can withstand losing 10% of your total revenue at one time and still survive...but usually not more than 10%.

Have You Managed Through A Downturn? Bankers like to see an owner or management team that has managed a business through bad times. During the 1990's, many companies participated in the longest period of sustained economic growth in the history of the country. Some business owners have never experienced a downturn in the economy. Others began to believe that good times would go on forever. One test of management's resourcefulness is to maintain profitability and positive cash flow when the economy hits the skids. Bankers are interested in companies that have the "smarts" and flexibility to weather rough seas as well as prospering when times are good.

Is There A Strong Management Team? This is similar but significantly different from "organization" noted above. The banker will base his final credit decision on how strong he feels the management team is. What does a "strong team" look like? This is a subjective call and each banker you speak to will explain this differently. A strong management team is hard to define; but the banker will know it when he or she sees it. He or she will also be interested in how much of the owner's personal financial resources are at risk. The more the better from the banker's perspective. He or she will judge that this means the owner is committed to the company's success.

What Is the Financial History of the Company? The financial history of any company is vital to the banker. He or she is especially interested in seeing if there has been a consistent record of profitability and positive cash flow. This will give him or her comfort that any loans have an excellent chance of being repaid. The banker is most interested in projections of future performance, too. You will be asked for month-by-month projections for the next 12 months, quarter-by-quarter for years two and three and yearly projections for years four and five. Precision and visibility about what the future holds drops off dramatically as you project out in time. Therefore, you can expect the banker to heavily discount your estimates for years 2 through 5. Projections must be done for the Operating Statement and the Balance Sheet. Only by doing both can you determine your cash flow. The most important aspect of your projections are the assumptions upon which the forecasts are based. You must put your assumptions in writing.

What Is the Company's Debt-to-Equity Ratio? What's this all about? The arithmetic is simple enough and the resultant answer is quite important to the banker in his or her decision process. A definition of this ratio is *the total debt of the company (all current liabilities and long term liabilities) compared to the company's equity (contributed capital plus retained earnings).* If the ratio is 1:1 you may be able to borrow on an unsecured basis. A ratio of greater than 1:1 up to 3:1 means you may be able to borrow on a secured, personally guaranteed basis. A ratio of greater than 3:1 means you may already be leveraged beyond the comfort level of most bankers. What about debt on your Balance Sheet that could be put into a subordinated (put in a secondary position) to bank debt such as loans from stockholders? Make sure you know how the banker will consider this type of debt when the Debt-to-Equity calculation is made. Take a look at your most recent Balance Sheet and determine whether or not your banker will think you are already too leveraged to handle any more debt.

The Character Issue. Banks want to do business with honorable people. You will be asked about your dealings with vendors, customers, employees and others in your business sphere. Is there a record of lawsuits filed by you and against you? Do suppliers consider you "slow pay"? Will the bank find liens recorded against you by contractors or tax authorities? Is there is history of frequent changes in banks, CPA firms and other professional advisors? A negative record in any of these areas will be a concern to the banker.

So, what makes for a "bankable" small business? There must be solid evidence that a well-defined business opportunity exists. The company will almost certainly have two or three years of profitable existence establishing a track record. It is in the growth phase of its corporate life cycle. There is a clear plan of action (written) to show where things are headed. The company is successfully managing its "operating cycle." There is strong and compelling evidence that new debt, along with interest, could be repaid. The banker is comfortable with management and believes he or she has open communication channels established. In addition, the informed borrower will present a well-defined idea about how much money is needed (be precise and realistic) and exactly what the money will be used for. The borrower should know how the loan process works inside the bank and if the bank has a centralized or decentralized loan approval method. Finally, you must develop banking relationships and seek loans *well before funds are actually needed*. This is an axiom of the banking business.

If you're "bankable," how much can be borrowed? How does the bank view various types of collateral (assets pledged to secure the repayment of the loan)?

Any bank will loan only as much money as they confidently believe can be repaid by the borrower. Repayment is always made in *cash*. There are five ways any company can generate cash to repay debt:

- From net earnings after taxes are paid.

- Liquidating fixed assets.

- Selling off inventory out of the operating cycle (referred to as "dumping," normally below cost).

- Shifting short-term debt to long term debt (referred to as "refinancing").

- Bringing in new equity capital.

Banks understand this paradigm and you must be clear about this, too, when a loan application is completed. The earning capacity of the business is very important to the banker. Most banks will want to see that a company's net after tax income during a specific time period (say, a year) is approximately one to one and one-half times the amount of principal and interest that must be repaid during the same time period. This is referred to as "coverage." Each bank may approach this differently. However, it is a good rule to follow for those seeking a loan.

What if you lose your ability to repay a loan? Banks require that all loans be collateralized by assets that will more than cover the amount of the borrowing. The last thing a bank wants to do is to come into a company to liquidate assets in order to repay a loan in default. However, *they are prepared to do just that.* Therefore, it is important to know how a bank will look at collateral that is offered by a potential borrower. What collateral will a bank accept? What is not acceptable? What discount will a bank apply to collateral it does accept?

The following list gives a good approximation of the percentage of the "book" value of collateral items that may be loaned by a bank. Please note—most banks will file a lien against all assets not just those pledged as collateral. The bank will often require a "negative pledge" that the company won't promise these same assets again to another lender.

Accounts Receivable (under 90 days)	65% - 85%
Finished Goods Inventory	20% - 40%
Work In Progress Inventory	Usually nothing.
Raw Material Inventory	10% - 30% if easily disposed of.
General Purpose Equipment	30% - 60%
Special Purpose Equipment	Little, if anything.
CD's, Securities (public companies)	60% - 90%
Real Estate—buildings	50% - 70% of appraised value.
Raw Land	10% - 30%, if anything.

The bank would prefer to have their loan repaid by funds generated in the business or with liquidated collateral owned by the business. However, most small business owners will also have to provide personal guarantees for loans made to the businesses they own and/or operate. This means that the personal assets of the owner—homes, autos, stocks, etc.—could be lost if the business fails and the business collateral is insufficient to repay the bank debt. If you are reluctant to personally guarantee loans, it raises questions in the banker's mind about your level of commitment and confidence in the business.

A word about the *costs* of borrowing money. We expect to pay interest, of course. Be aware that you may also be charged a *standby fee*, compensation to the bank for committing their funds to your loan. There may also be *loan fees* for processing the paperwork and setting up your account. You may incur *legal fees* in reviewing the loan documents required by the bank. There may also be a requirement that you keep *compensating balances* on deposit. These are minimum deposit levels required by the bank, money that you are keeping in the bank without earning interest. Finally, you could face substantial *accounting fees* if the bank insists that your financial statements be reviewed or audited as a condition of granting a loan. Be very clear about these costs prior to entering into any agreements.

A borrower must understand that banks are governed by a complex set of laws designed to protect their depositors' money. Banks are adverse to risk and require a lot of information before committing to loan money. Companies wishing to borrow from a bank must do a complete job of preparing the documents required in a lending transaction. Business plans, historical financial statements, tax returns of the company and the owner and financial projections for the company are but a few of the items. Virtually all information required is data that the business owner *should have readily available* if the business is being properly managed. Finally, the potential borrower must produce a loan proposal that spells out the following things.

Summary. How much money do you need? What will the money be used for? When is the money needed? How will it be repaid?

Management Profiles. Provide resumes on the business owners and all key personnel.

Business Description. Briefly tell the bank what the business does, what makes the company unique and what is its market niche.

Financial Projections. They *must* be realistic. It is usually wise to show an "optimistic-realistic-pessimistic" scenario so the bank recognizes you have thought about a fallback plan.

Financial Statements. Provide as much history as you can. It is better if the statements have been compiled, reviewed or audited by an outside CPA firm. Compare financial results against industry standards. (Refer to Robert Morris Associates or Standard & Poors Financial Statement Studies for industry data. This requires that you know your company's Standard Industry Classification—SIC—code number).

Purpose for the Loan. Be very specific here; no broad generalities permitted.

Amount of the Loan. How much money are you seeking to borrow?

Repayment Plans. You must show exactly how the loan and the interest can be repaid. If the loan's purpose is to acquire a specific asset, show how that asset will generate cash to repay the loan. Remember, the bank is looking for "coverage" of interest and principal by a factor of 1X to 1.5X, usually. Also, make sure you are offering the bank "two ways out" of the loan in case insufficient cash is generated in the business to repay the debt. Finally, and most importantly, be candid throughout your loan proposal.

What if you are turned down for bank credit? Make sure you find out why you were rejected. There are other sources of money that may be willing to help you. Some businesses turn to factoring, asset-based lenders, leasing companies or even friends or relatives. Seeking a bank loan requires careful preparation and a thorough understanding of how the loan process works and how bankers operate. If you do obtain bank credit, make sure you manage your banking relationship effectively. A crucial final point: keep your banker informed about how your company is doing. Nothing will upset a banker more than to be "surprised" with news that wasn't expected.

MINDING YOUR BUSINESS

You are the owner or manager of a small business. Even though you don't have a lot of digits on your financial statements, there seems to be an endless number of things for you to keep track of, to monitor and to control. The ubiquitous personal computer and access to the Internet may actually be complicating the process. There is *so much* data and information available. What are the absolutely key things you must track? Given the time pressure imposed by *operating* your company, how do you prioritize *what* to monitor and *when* to do it? This chapter will address these issues and provide some specific recommendations about how to set up and maintain an oversight system in your company.

Let's begin by stating a complicating condition. Many owners/managers of small businesses are not comfortable reading and understanding standard financial reports. Assuming that you are producing monthly financial statements for your business, the Operating Statement (also referred to as Profit and Loss Statement) can appear to be endless columns of numbers with little meaning. Just to survive, you have learned to understand the general relationship between Sales, Cost of Sales, Monthly Expenses and how they combine to produce a Profit (hopefully). When your bookkeeper or accountant begins talking to you about inadequate accruals of selling expenses, the amount of your bad debt expenses and non-cash expenses like depreciation, some of you glaze over slightly. You may experience a vague uneasiness when you're not *absolutely sure* what this means to your business. The Balance Sheet creates even more uncertainty. Again, you know that Assets are "good" because they are things you *own*. Liabilities are "bad" since this is money you *owe*. The difference between Assets and Liabilities represents Net Worth, the *accounting* value of the business. Fine, up 'till now. Once again, the accountant begins talking to you about Inventory Valuation, the adequacy of warranty expense reserves and Working Capital, the proper allocation of debt into Current Portion and Long Term, Schedule M adjustments for your LIFO inventory, Deferred Taxes, etc. You're nodding your head as if everything being said is perfectly clear. On a parallel track in your mind, you are thinking, "I'm not dumb, but I just don't get all this accounting stuff. It really bothers me that there are things going on in my business that *I don't thoroughly understand.*" We haven't even gotten to the Cash Flow Statement yet so we'll save that for a later time.

If you see a little of yourself in the story told above, don't fret too much. Many business owners have mastered the accounting intricacies of their operations. They are probably not the ones reading this chapter. We are directing our advice to those who need to have a business control road map without becoming accounting wizards. There is a scoreboard for every business. We need to know how to read the scoreboard to understand whether we are winning or losing our particular game. For those of you with a background in engineering, sales, marketing or production we hope to provide a primer for scoreboard reading in the fascinating world of business performance measurement.

Key Success Factors.

You probably started or acquired your business. If you have achieved any level of success so far, it is surely the result of you doing a few key things very well and avoiding some fundamental errors. If it were easy to identify these key success factors then everybody would start a small business and most would be prosperous. But, as you already know, it is often difficult to spot the right buttons to push. The business world is full of ambiguity, shades of gray and conflicting signals. It is easy to make a mistake with a new product introduction, marketing program, pricing decision or site selection. To "get it right" is tough. Every decision hinges on multiple factors. To see through the haze, balance your available resources and determine the 3-4 absolutely crucial things to do is fundamental to most business success. You have probably done this. Looking back, you may say, "What I did in that situation shaped my overall business model. I was guessing at the time. Fortunately, it turned out OK." Fair enough. Most of us don't have brilliant insight or a reliable crystal ball to see the end result of our decisions. But, now comes the hard part. If you haven't articulated the *key success factors* for your business, *do it now.* Try rising up to the big picture level of 40,000 feet. There you can examine those crucial items that have contributed to your success. One factor might be a marketing decision to utilize one sales channel versus another. Another could be a product decision regarding "features versus price" that has given you a competitive advantage. A third might be investment in special equipment. Maybe you have done a great job recruiting and retaining top-notch people. Whatever the factors are, *write them down.* Recognize their importance to your success. Don't lose sight of these factors as your business grows and changes. Make sure that your employees and colleagues know and understand the importance of keeping alive the traditional success factors in your business. If you can't figure out what the *key success factors* have been for you, that spells trouble. By drifting in a commercial river allowing the current to control your final destination, you may be surprised by the steep waterfall around the next bend. When faced with uncertainty about these factors, ask your best customers. They can tell you, from their perspective, what has made your company successful up till now.

Keeping Track of Business Operations.

Key Success Factors are one thing. They are best seen from 40,000 feet. To stay in touch with the details of your business requires that you get down to treetop level for a closer look. What should you monitor? There isn't enough time or energy to examine everything. Determining the *Key Operational Factors* is not difficult. Some you will find on your financial statements. Others are available from other parts of your business operations. Here are some suggestions for the vital signs that you need to keep track of.

> *Revenue/Backlog.* How are sales? Compared to last week, last month, last quarter last year, the current budget...how are we doing? If you have an order cycle of longer than 24 hours (because you manufacture or fabricate your products) how are incoming orders and backlog? Backlog is defined as firm orders in house that are not yet shipped. Typical production facilities work most efficiently when the open order file (backlog) permits a smooth production schedule. For example, if your order cycle is one month (from receipt of a customer P.O. to shipment and invoicing of the order) you may have learned that a minimum order backlog of 1-2 months allows you to produce the goods in the most cost-effective manner. This varies widely by industry and because of competitive pressures. You need to figure this out for your operation. The old saying is "Nothing happens until somebody sells something." That is true. Having a good

handle on your current revenue (today's invoiced products and services) and future revenue (existing backlog) is an important component of your monitoring system.

Cost of Sales. Whether you provide services, manufacture products or distribute goods, you incur costs to generate every dollar of sales revenue. The difference between net revenue generated and the cost directly associated with this revenue is called Gross Profit or Gross Margin. These costs are considered variable since they are not incurred except to generate a sales dollar. Many so-called business experts say that the true test of effective management is the ability to enhance gross profit. This is often *very* hard to do. Costs of labor, fringe benefits, materials, supplies, outside services, freight…in short, the costs of producing revenue…seem to escalate continuously. Meanwhile, competitive pressures keep selling prices depressed. Most business owners feel this price-cost squeeze on a daily basis. Because it is so crucial, gross profit must be monitored regularly. When deterioration of margin is discovered, the effective manager must respond decisively.

"Common Size" Cost Control. Many costs in a business *appear* to be fixed, i.e., they routinely occur regardless of increases or decreases in sales. Items like rent, insurance, telephone, office salaries, utilities and a host of other categories relentlessly appear in the "to be paid" file. *In the long run,* all costs are variable but for purposes of this discussion we assume that the recurring selling, general and administrative costs in your business are fixed. How are these costs monitored and controlled? Try using a technique called a "common size" profit and loss statement. Instead of dollar amounts, all costs are calculated as a percentage of net sales revenue. Regardless of dollar amount, "Net Revenue" will always be 100.0%. Below the net revenue line, all costs are expressed as a percentage of net sales. When monthly figures are presented side-by-side using a spreadsheet program, you will see revealing trends regarding your costs.

Times Interest Earned. If you are borrowing money (who isn't at one time or another) you must keep track whether earnings are enough to cover interest payments. Most commercial lenders refer to this as "coverage." Essentially, your net income after taxes in any period should equal 1.0-1.5 times the amount of principal and interest you must repay during the same period. While principal payments *may* be negotiable during a rough stretch, interest payments *never* are. Therefore, you should monitor Times Interest Earned closely. To calculate, divide Net Income after Tax Provision on your Operating Statement by Interest Expense. You shouldn't feel comfortable unless result is 2.0 or more.

Revenue Per Employee (RPE). You frequently hear prominent economists or the Chairman of the Federal Reserve speak about "improvements in worker productivity." This is seen as a healthy economic signal that promotes corporate profits and justifies non-inflationary wage increases. Whether macroeconomics (the global/national village) or microeconomics (your company), increasing productivity is good. You may not have the knowledge or resources to calculate productivity using classic economic models. Don't despair. By figuring your Net Revenue per each employee and comparing these results over time, you have created a "poor person's" productivity measurement. The arithmetic is simple: divide sales by the number of people working for you. You can tweak this by figuring RPE for production workers, sales and administrative personnel or company wide. Higher RPE says you are improving your processes, eliminating waste and operating smarter. Worsening RPE may indicate excessive personnel, inefficiencies or sloppy procedures. Keep track of this faithfully as a good indication about the general health of your operation.

Accounts Receivable Aging and Days Sales Outstanding. Most industrial companies offer credit terms as part of their sales strategy. That creates interest free loans to customers known as Accounts Receivable. This can become a significant asset and must be carefully monitored because it represents future cash coming into the business. You should track Accounts Receivable two ways. First, an aging report should be created (usually twice a month) showing amounts current, up to 30, 60 or 90 days past due and over 90 days past due. Some one in your organization must be responsible for a *specific* collection plan on each invoice over 60 days past due. Track that action plan on a *daily* basis. Accounts Receivable over 90 days past due is seldom collectible. A second way to track Accounts Receivable is using Days Sales Outstanding. To calculate, annualize your net credit sales revenue (sales in N months divided by N and multiplied by 12) and divide by 360. This result is the net credit sales per day based on a 360-day year. Total Accounts Receivable should be divided by credit sales per day to show how many days of sales are in Accounts Receivable. Ideally, the result should be very close to your normal credit terms, say, 30 days. If the DSO begins creeping more than 25% greater than terms, you may have a problem. Check the DSO monthly and insist on corrective action when it exceeds reasonable boundaries.

Inventory Turnover. Another key asset for most industrial companies is inventory. Whether as raw material, component parts, work-in-process or finished goods, inventory must be regularly monitored. Control should extend to count accuracy, potential obsolescence, excessive quantities and valuation accuracy. No single asset category can cause more grief for the business owner than inventory. You need enough to fill orders and to create smooth production flow. You don't want too much because that absorbs cash and takes space. One measurement tool is Inventory Turnover. To calculate, annualize sales (N months of sales divided by N multiplied by 12) and divide this result by the total value of inventory. This tells you the number of times your inventory is turning over in a year based on annual sales. For example, if annual sales are $4.0 Million and you have $1.0 Million of inventory, turnover is 4 times. How often should inventory turn over? It depends on the complexity of your manufacturing process, the lead-time to acquire needed materials and the mix of your inventory categories. Refer to Robert Morris Associates Financial Statement Profiles or Standard & Poors (both found on the Internet) for turnover statistics in your industry and for your size of business. Inventory Turnover should be monitored monthly and displayed on a spreadsheet program so trends can be spotted.

Cash. Well, DUH! Most business owners reflexively say "Cash flow is key to my success." True enough. The fact that many owners can't construct a Cash Flow Statement (Sources and Uses of Funds) means we need to offer some helping mechanisms to monitor cash flow. I've heard it said (by my own spouse), "If the business is doing so well, how come we never have any cash?" Business owners tend to forget the negative impact on cash caused by the buildup of Accounts Receivable and Inventory. Cash is a scarce commodity in most businesses. You need to keep a minimum amount on hand to cover operational requirements. Additional amounts must be *available* to insure smooth flowing production, timely payment of payrolls, taxes and vendor invoices. Whether the cash reserves are self generated (highly preferable) or provided by a line of credit is somewhat moot. We must have (or be able to obtain) enough cash to sustain our current level of business activity. So, how much is enough? Each situation will be unique. However, you want to have ready cash for at least one gross payroll, 2-3 weeks of Accounts Payable and enough to cover special payments that are imminent. Work out your own requirements and watch the balances closely. What about excess cash? Sometimes a company will accumulate cash far beyond their current needs. It's warm and fuzzy to have a cushion like this. But, make sure it is deposited in an interest bearing account. If you have short-term debt that carries an interest cost beyond what your funds can earn, consider using the excess cash to pay off debt. That is a prudent use of resources. Why pay, say, 10% interest on debt when you have excess funds that can only earn, say, 6%? A payoff puts you ahead of the game at least by the interest rate spread.

Working Capital and the Quick Ratio. These measurements are an extension of Cash control. Working Capital is defined as *Current Assets minus Current Liabilities* as found on the Balance Sheet. It represents the short term capital needed to operate your business. The closer Working Capital comes to zero, the tighter your Cash Flow will be. Therefore, more Working Capital is always better than less. Monitor this number monthly. The Quick Ratio (also called the Acid Test Ratio) is a variation. Subtract Inventory from Current Assets. Now subtract Current Liabilities. This measures cash and equivalents on the Asset side that are available to meet short-term debt on the Liabilities side. A ratio of 1:1 is adequate. Anything less should make you somewhat nervous. It says you don't have enough short-term assets to cover your short-term liabilities.

The Mechanics of Management Control and Monitoring.

Most managers want a simple and concise method for monitoring things under their responsibility. Over the years, I have seen many "Flash Reports" developed by successful managers. In every case, the Flash Report displays on one 8-1/2" X 11" page the key data to be monitored by senior executives. Consider the crucial operational data you would like to see daily, weekly and monthly. Each company's Flash Report must be uniquely designed to review the most important operational factors for that specific business. Yours will be different from everyone else's. However, you may find that you can borrow ideas from others. The key to producing an effective Flash Report is timeliness and the understanding that the Boss is reviewing this information *everyday*. Here are just a few examples of what you might see on a daily Flash Report.

- Today's date
- Number of working days left in the month
- Net sales today and month to date
- Orders booked today and month to date
- Backlog of unshipped orders
- An aging of the order backlog in one week segments
- Cash collected today and month to date
- Accounts receivable balance and aging report
- Accounts payable balance and aging report
- Headcount by each department
- Cash balances and the bank loan available to borrow
- Value of products completed and transferred to finished goods inventory

The Use of Ratios on Monthly Financial Statements

Financial statements are often presented to business owners with little analysis of what the numbers really mean. Adding important business ratios to the financial statements could make them more meaningful. Following are some examples of additional ratios that might give more insight to the reader of monthly reports.

Return on Assets. Profits after Tax Provision divided by Total Assets. This gives a quick assessment of how efficiently the firm uses its assets.

Return on Sales. Profits after Tax Provision divided by Net Sales. This gives a quick assessment of the profitability of the operation.

Return on Equity. Profits after Tax Provision divided by Shareholder's equity. This gives a quick assessment of the return on stockholder's investment.

Current Ratio. Current Assets divided by Current Liabilities. Indicates the basic liquidity of the firm. Should be about 2:1.

Debt to Equity. Current Liabilities plus Long Term Debt divided by Shareholder's equity. This indicates how much the firm relies on debt versus equity for funding.

This represents just a handful of the many financial ratios commonly used. You need to employ the ones that help you control and monitor your business. Use them in a way that leads you to the details of what you must know and where you must intervene.

A Schedule—What to Monitor and When.

Consider the following schedule for monitoring performance. Adjust it to meet your specific needs and the changing nature of your business operations.

Information to Monitor	Daily	Weekly	Monthly	Yearly
Cash on Hand/Line of Credit availability	XXX			
Revenue/Order Backlog	XXX			
Accounts Receivable Aging/Collection Action Plan		XXX		
Cost of Sales - Components			XXX	
Cost Control - Period Expenses and Other Expenses			XXX	
Interest Expense "Coverage" - Times Interest Earned			XXX	
Revenue Per Employee			XXX	
Inventory - Turnover, Excess Quantities, Obsolesence			XXX	
Working Capital & Quick (Acid Test) Ratio			XXX	
Review All Financial Reports			XXX	
Review Selected Financial Ratios			XXX	
Key Success Factors				XXX

While monitoring performance is important, you must also consider the role played by the planning and budgeting function. Without comparing actual results to budgeted standards, you will be missing a key element of control. Merely looking at actual results to "see how things are going" is insufficient. You really want to see how performance compares to plan. This means that a senior management commitment to yearly planning must be understood throughout the organization.

CALCULATING CASH FLOW

When one asks the owner of a small business, "What's the most important thing in your business?" the answer is often, "Cash flow." It is axiomatic that there must be an adequate supply of cash for any business to survive. Short-term obligations are almost always paid in cash. If you don't have enough cash, the viability of the business is threatened. This is a fundamental and obvious fact. Yet, many small business owners may have a difficult time calculating the cash flow in their companies. The purpose of this chapter is to explain, in simple and straightforward language and formulae, how to calculate cash flow.

Every business has a rhythm. There is a continuous stream of events that may increase or decrease the available balance of cash. What are the events that *increase* cash?

Collection of Accounts Receivable. When customers pay the invoices you have rendered to them and the collections are deposited in the bank.

Cash Register Receipts. If you have a retail business, cash (and perhaps debit and credit card charges) is deposited at the end of each workday.

Borrowing or Capital Infusion. Loans from yourself, friends, banks and/or other financial institutions increase your cash. New equity investment from you or outside investors does the same. While this may be an important source of cash, we will not include these funds in actual cash flow calculations. The reasons for this will be explained later.

Sale of Fixed Assets. Surplus equipment or rolling stock may be sold to generate cash.

What events *decrease* cash?

Acquisition of Materials. Cash is decreased when we acquire and pay for materials and/or services needed to produce our products.

Employee Costs. Meeting the periodic payroll, paying the associated taxes and paying for employee benefit programs decreases cash.

Periodic Expenses. All companies have a host of expenses like rent, utilities, insurance, interest, sales and marketing expenses, principal payments on debt, taxes and others, all of which decrease cash.

Acquisition of Fixed Assets. New machinery, rolling stock, building improvements, etc. all decrease cash as they are paid for.

Payment of Dividends to Shareholders. A company may periodically make dividend payments to shareholders.

It is important to note that actual increase or decrease in cash often does not coincide with the accounting transaction itself. For example, the shipment of a product and the rendering of an invoice increases Sales on the income statement and Accounts Receivable on the balance sheet. However, cash may not be collected from the customer until 30, 60 or 90 days later. Similarly, the purchase of raw material will increase the Inventory and Accounts Payable accounts on the balance sheet but you may not pay the vendor invoice for 30-45 days. In another case a new truck purchased for cash now may be set up on the balance sheet as a Fixed Asset to be depreciated down to residual value over 3-4 years. Understanding *timing* is crucial to calculating accurate cash flow statements. Finally, certain expenses posted to the income statement are non-cash items. Examples are Depreciation and/or Amortization. While these items are treated as operating expenses that reduce Pre-tax Profit on the income statement, they do not have a cash effect on the business.

So, what is cash flow? How is cash flow defined? It's surprising to note that even financial experts may differ on a definition for cash flow. You will often hear, or read, that cash flow is composed of three elements: cash from *operations*, cash from *investments* and cash from *financing*. This chapter places emphasis on the first two and we'll leave financing for a later discussion. No matter what definition is applied, the small business owner needs to know the following information.

- What cash is being generated (or used) by the operations of the company?
- What changes in assets and/or liabilities are providing or using cash?
- Is my current cash flow adequate to support my actual and planned level of operations?
- If cash flow is not adequate how much additional cash is required?
- Where do I find this additional financing and how much will it cost me?

Here is a simple step-by-step formula to do the calculations required.

CASH FLOW FROM OPERATIONS

Profit after Tax (from the Income Statement)

\+   Depreciation and Amortization

+/-   Working Capital Changes

Changes in Current Assets (increases are negative and decreases are positive)

Accounts Receivable

Inventory

Prepaid Expenses

Other current assets

Changes in Current Liabilities (increases are positive and decreases are negative)

Accounts Payable

Taxes Payable

Accrued Liabilities

Other current liabilities (excluding borrowings)

=   *Net Cash Flow Provided (Used) By Operations*

CASH FLOW FROM INVESTMENT

-     Net Investment in new Fixed Assets

-     Other Investments

=   *Net Cash Flow Provided (Used) By Investment*

CASH FLOW FOR THE PERIOD (INVESTMENT PLUS OPERATING FLOWS)

+   Beginning Cash Balance

-     Desired Ending Cash Balance

=   *Net Cash Surplus/(Required)*

Study this simple formula carefully. First, you will note that Depreciation and/or Amortization is added back to Profit after Tax to reflect the non-cash nature of Depreciation. The resultant answer is *a part of the cash flow from operations*. Next you will see that increases in asset accounts cause a decrease in cash. If Accounts Receivable, Inventory, Deposits, Fixed Assets or other asset accounts increase period to period, this will use cash. Conversely, increases in liability accounts cause an increase in cash. If Accounts Payable, Taxes Payable or other liabilities (excluding short-term loans or equity capital) increase period to period, this will provide cash. Adjustments to the current asset and current liability accounts, when added to the Income cash flows, produces the *Net Operating Cash Provided (Used) By Operations*. The actual Beginning Cash Balance is added to the calculated Net Cash Flow. From the sum of these numbers, subtract a Desired Ending Cash Balance. The result is the *Net Cash Surplus/Required* representing the extra cash available or what is required to fund the operation.

If there is surplus cash, that money can be used to reduce short-term borrowings. If there is no debt to retire, the surplus may be used to buy financial instruments, declare a dividend for the equity holders or for various company growth plans. On the other hand, if there is a cash deficit it must be determined how this will be covered and at what cost.

The Desired Ending Cash Balance should not be a number plucked out of the air. Some business owners like the security of having lots of cash available. Others may often be starved for cash and don't have that luxury. To determine how much cash to have on hand is a unique calculation for every company. Things to consider might be your next gross payroll, one month of accounts payable, a reserve for fixed payments to be made during the next month, etc. You will be fortunate if you have enough cash reserves to create an Ending Cash Balance. On the other hand, it is not wise to keep large amounts of cash available if they can be put to better use. This is a subjective decision that needs a good deal of careful analysis.

Why aren't we considering Cash Provided by Financing? The simple answer is that the business owner needs to know the cash flow from his or her operations and investment activity first. This is what is happening inside his or her company. Once that is determined, a judgment can be made about bringing in outside funds including the costs, risks and rewards of doing so. It is important not to begin counting on outside investment just to make your cash flow positive.

The simplified spread sheet below shows a quarter-ending financial report of key cash flow accounts. It also shows a three month projection so that cash flow can be estimated for the upcoming quarter. Note the period-to-period comparisons shown. It is the key to understanding the formula. The formula mentions "increases" in asset and liability accounts. Increases from what? From the projected or actual numbers in the prior period. By studying these accounts we see the activity that increases or decreases our cash flow. The purpose of the example is to determine the *Net Cash Surplus/Required* for each projected month and the total for the upcoming quarter. Not considered is the requirement for a cash balance needed to fund company operations. Should management want to keep, say, $40,000 on hand, that amount must be added to the requirement shown below. Please note the discussion in the paragraph directly above.

Dollar Amounts: 000's Omitted								
–	Actual Quarter	Proj. Mo. 1	C/F	Proj. Mo. 2	C/F	Proj. Mo. 3	C/F	C/F Quarter
Profit, After Tax	$90	$35		$40		$45		$120
Add: Depreciation	$10	$10		$10		$11		$31
Cash Flow, Operations	$100	$45	$45	$50	$50	$56	$56	$151
Accounts Receivable	$150	$165	($15)	$170	($5)	$175	($5)	($25)
Inventory	$200	$205	($5)	$210	($5)	$215	($5)	($15)
Fixed Assets	$600	$600		$700	($100)	$700		($100)
Accounts Payable	$125	$130	$5	$130		$140	$10	$15
Taxes Payable	$85	$50	($35)	$40	($10)	$30	($10)	($55)
Net Cash Flow			($5)		($70)		$46	($29)
Cash Surplus/(Required)			($5)		($70)		$46	($29)

This example should also be studied carefully. Note that Accounts Receivable and Inventory are expected to increase each month. This is treated as a *use* of cash. Accounts Payable in Month 1 was projected to be higher than the Actual results. This is treated as a *source* of cash. Why? The theory is that increased credit extended to the company by its vendors is the same as an interest free loan. The company plans to pay down the tax liability. This is a *use* of cash. There is a plan to add a substantial amount to Fixed Assets in Month 2. Again, this is a *use* of cash. Please find all the similar increases and decreases in accounts month-to-month and satisfy yourself that you thoroughly understand the formula. Finally, the far right column summarizes the Cash Flow for the projected quarter. The very last number shows that, given these projections, the company's net Cash Flow will be a negative $29,000. Remember, this does not include any cash-on-hand requirement. Either this money must be borrowed, new equity invested (this is what is called *cash flow from financing*) or there must be restrictions on the growth of assets or the reduction of liabilities during the period. Where do we find lenders or investors willing to put their cash into our business? How much will it cost us to obtain these funds? This Cash Flow report (sometimes referred to as a Sources and Uses of Cash report) can be very useful for planning. In addition, it can be prepared along with an Income (or Operating) Statement and Balance Sheet each month to provide management with another element in a financial "tool kit" to effectively conduct the business.

The lack of adequate cash has sunk many a business. Surprisingly, it is often during periods of substantial growth when companies find themselves starved for cash. Rapid increases in Accounts Receivable and Inventory can suck cash out of a company, even one that is operating profitably. Reports indicate that Chapter 11 bankruptcy filings often occur in the year following the largest sales increases in a company's history.

The method of determining Cash Flow described in this monograph requires complete Income Statements and Balance Sheets. Other methods of determining net cash flow are available. For example, one can list—in detail—all projected outflows and inflows of cash for the time period being forecasted. Whatever method you choose, make Cash Flow measurement and projection a part of your financial reporting system

WHAT'S THE "BREAKEVEN POINT" FOR YOUR BUSINESS?

What is the "Breakeven Point?" It is the point where net sales revenue is enough to cover costs thus producing neither a loss nor a profit. To create a simple model, assume all costs are categorized as *variable* or *fixed*. Therefore, *sales* minus *variable costs* equals *gross profit* or *gross margin*. *Gross profit* minus *fixed costs* equals pre-tax *operating profit* or *loss*.

Consider the simplified Operating Statement for the ABC Company.

For the Year Ending 12/31/XX	
Net Sales Revenue	$2,400,000
All Variable Costs associated with producing	
The Net Sales Revenue	$1,800,000
Gross Profit/Margin	$ 600,000
Gross Profit/Margin %	25%
All Fixed (Period) Expenses for the same period	$ 800,000
Net Operating Profit or Loss	($ 200,000)

As noted, ABC Company experienced an operating loss for the year. Management is trying to determine how to eliminate this loss (at a minimum) during the next year.

What actions can management take to solve this problem? Essentially, they have three options: (1) Increase Net Sales Revenue; (2) Improve the Gross

Profit Margin; (3) Reduce Fixed costs. They can work on each of these options individually or blend their efforts to improve each area of the business.

How much improvement is needed in each available option so that ABC Company reaches breakeven next year? The following formulae can be used to calculate the answers assuming the results from the prior period will remain the same for the next year.

What level of SALES is needed to reach breakeven?

- Divide the Fixed Costs by the Gross Profit percentage.

- $800,000 divided by .25 (25%) = $3,200,000.

- Assuming Gross Profit remains at 25% and Fixed Costs remain at $800,000, Net Sales Revenue must increase to $3,200,000 to breakeven.

What level of GROSS PROFIT percentage must we achieve to reach breakeven?

- Divide the Fixed Costs by the Net Sales Revenue.

- $800,000 divided by $2,400,000 = 33%.

- Assuming Fixed Costs remain at $800,000 and Sales remain at $2,400,000, the Gross Profit percentage must improve to 33% to achieve breakeven.

What level of FIXED COSTS must we achieve to reach breakeven?

- Multiply the Net Sales Revenue by the Gross Profit percentage.

- $2,400,000 multiplied by .25 (25%) = $600,000.

- Assuming Sales remain at $2,400,000 and Gross Profit percentage remains at 25%, the Fixed Costs must be reduced to $600,000 in order to achieve breakeven.

Using these simple equations, management can quickly calculate what effect increased sales, improved gross margin percentages or fixed cost reduction will mean to their breakeven point. Which is easier to accomplish—raising revenue, improving margins or cutting fixed costs? By playing "what if" management can experiment with different plans until they settle on a strategy that is achievable. This analysis technique is also helpful in product pricing strategies. It is easy to see how much you can reduce your gross margin percentage before the sale becomes unprofitable.

Admittedly, the analysis explained above is simplistic. Complicating factors include the difficulty of determining what costs are variable with the level of sales. In addition, there are really no fixed costs *in the long run*. In other words, even costs which appear to be permanent and unchangeable can be modified (reduced) over time. Costs, both variable and fixed, don't necessarily move linearly with revenue. Costs often experience step increases. Our model does not consider these possibilities.

In spite of these factors, this breakeven model can be very useful especially for small business owners who lack sophisticated financial reporting systems or the skills to apply more complex analysis to their business operations. A thorough understanding of breakeven analysis, particularly the business levers that can be adjusted to improve performance, should be a part of every business manager's financial toolkit.

SHOULD I LEASE OR BUY A CORPORATE FACILITY?

Assume you are in charge of making a decision about whether to lease or purchase a facility to house your corporation. What information is relevant to the decision? What economic factors must be considered? What fundamental assumptions must be postulated? Following is a generalized and high level decision model that can be used to answer these questions.

Your company needs 100,000 sq. ft. of space. It has been determined that this amount of space will be adequate for many years into the future. Your search for a facility has discovered that space of this type is currently available for a monthly lease cost of $.30 per square foot on a "triple net" basis. The term "triple net" means that the lessee of the building is responsible for all *insurance, maintenance* and *taxes* in addition to the monthly lease. Therefore, the cost to lease this facility is $30,000 per month (100,000 sq. ft. X $.30/sq. ft.) or $360,000 per year in addition to insurance, maintenance and taxes. You have calculated that your company could absorb this amount of cost for the facility.

Instead of leasing this facility, it might be possible to buy an appropriate amount of land and build your own building. Your investigation has determined that you would need 225,000 sq. ft of land in order to build a 100,000 sq. ft building. Current land costs are about $5 per sq. ft. and a building suitable for your requirements can be erected for $20 per sq. ft. Therefore, your costs to acquire the land and build a facility are as follows:

225,000 sq. ft. of land	@$5/sq. ft	=$1,125,000
100,000 sq. ft. of building	@$20/sq. ft	=$2,000,000
Total cost of construction		$3,125,000

Your company does not have the cash to buy the land and build a building. It would be necessary to borrow the money to execute this alternative. The question is: Can the money be borrowed? You would plan to build a general-purpose building and could afford to make a mortgage payment of $30,000 per month.

How is commercial real estate valued? This is important since any lender you might approach to loan you money to build wants to have a clear understanding of collateral available to secure a loan. In general, commercial real estate is valued three ways:

Cost Basis. This method is based on determining what it would cost to duplicate an existing building based on today's construction costs.

Comparables. This method examines recent leases and/or purchases of buildings in the area that are generally the same size and offering the same amenities. The assumption is that willing buyers and willing sellers with sufficient and equal knowledge negotiated a Fair Market Value price for the facility.

Capitalization of Earnings. This is the most commonly used valuation method. Gross yearly rents are discounted by assumed *management fees* and *vacancy rates* to arrive at a figure called "Net Operating Income." A *capitalization rate* is then applied to the Net Operating Income to determine the value of the building *through the eyes of an investor or lender.*

The Capitalization of Earnings method uses several factors that must be clearly understood.

Management Fees. Typically, gross rent will be reduced by 3% to reflect the assumed cost of managing the property.

Vacancy Rate. Gross rent will also be reduced by 5% to reflect the presumption that the facility will be vacant at least 5% of the time it is available for rent.

Capitalization Rate. This is the rate of return on invested capital that the lender will deem to be satisfactory *given the current economic conditions.* That number is usually a percentage about 2-1/2 to 5 points above the interest rates currently being paid on 30-year U.S. Treasury bills.

The value of real estate in general and the capitalization rate specifically are directly and materially influenced by interest rates. When economic times are good, interest rates are relatively low and money to lend is plentiful, lenders will be satisfied with a lower rate of return. When the economic situation is reversed meaning high interest rates and a scarcer supply of money, lenders will demand a higher rate of return. For purposes of this high level model we will assume a capitalization rate of 8% in "good" times and 12% in "bad" economic times.

Using this information, let us return to our example of a building that would lease for $360,000 per year in gross rent. What value would a lender assign to this building? First, the gross rent would be reduced by 3% for management fees ($360,000 X .03 = $10,800) and 5% for a vacancy factor ($360,000 X .05 = $18,000). The gross rent less the management fees and vacancy rate equals $331,200, a result that is referred to as "Net Operating Income." This number divided by the capitalization rate will determine the lender's *perception* of value. Given the two extremes of our model ("good" times and "bad" times) we can see how a lender might value the Net Operating Income earnings stream using two possible capitalization rates.

- "Good" times: $331,200 divided by 8% (required   = $4,140,000 rate of return)

- "Bad" times: $331,200 divided by 12% (required   = $2,760,000 rate of return)

How is this information useful to us? Assume you presented a proposal to your banker to lend you money to buy land and build a building that produced $360,000 in yearly gross rent. From the example above, you can see that the banker might value this building...in good times...at $4,140,000. Further, he might be willing to lend you about 75% of the value, i.e., $3,105,000. Since we determined that we could build this building for $3,125,000, only about $20,000 of equity would be required to acquire the facility instead of leasing. If that loan could be arranged and paid off on a 30-year schedule at 10% interest rate, the monthly payment would be approximately $27,250—less than the $30,000 monthly lease. Using the same criteria, it is also easy to see that borrowing and building in "bad" economic times would probably not be possible due to lower collateral values. A 75% loan on a building valued at $2,760,000 would leave you over $1 Million short of the funds needed to buy land and construct the building.

A 30-year amortization schedule was used in this example to demonstrate that monthly lease or mortgage payments were quite similar. Examination of a 30-year amortization schedule on the $3,105,000 mortgage shows that there would be little reduction of principal for well over 20 years. In other words, the monthly payment is mostly interest. That means the facility remains highly leveraged with debt for a long time. Simply put, this might be a reasonable tax decision but a poor economic decision. On the other hand, a 15-year amortization schedule on the same mortgage requires a monthly payment of approximately $33,400. If one can afford the higher monthly payments, leverage is reduced much faster. By year 8, the principal portion of each payment exceeds interest. The building owners soon will possess a valuable asset free from debt. Assuming a nominal rate of inflation, this asset is actually growing in value over time. A debt free real estate investment is, therefore, a reliable way of building wealth, whether corporate or individual.

Business people often say, "I have to lease a facility since I don't have the resources to build." This is not necessarily true. It may be possible to borrow all, or most, of the cost of acquiring land and building a building *depending on the current economic conditions.* Make sure you understand the capitalization rates currently being used by lenders. As described above, it may be that low interest rates and plentiful money will permit a lender to accept a lower rate of return on his capital. In addition, don't confuse capitalization rates (which address the question of rates of return on invested capital) with interest rates (which are the percentage rates of rent on borrowed money).

In summary, the key concepts to internalize from this chapter are:

- The difference between Gross Rent and Net Operating Income.

- The three basic ways to value Real Estate.

- Why capitalization rates can vary between good and bad economic times.

- The general way capitalization rates are determined.
- The difference between capitalization rates, interest rates and discount rates.

DISCOURAGING FRAUD AND EMBEZZLEMENT IN SMALL BUSINESSES

Many small or emerging businesses must rely on a very limited staff—often just one person—to complete all accounting transactions that must be accomplished. Everything from opening the mail, making deposits, processing accounts payable, invoicing, maintaining accounts receivable, handling payroll and petty cash is frequently entrusted to a single individual. We also find many small companies with very basic computer software systems that do not provide adequate audit trails. While the great majority of people will handle these financial responsibilities conscientiously and with scrupulous honesty, some will not. Unfortunately, the *opportunity* for dishonesty is greatly magnified in small companies where one person has unrestricted access to the means of defalcation. There are just too many stories of theft and embezzlement from business organizations to ignore the need for prudent, effective controls.

The purpose of this chapter is to outline a series of simple, practical steps any business owner can take to thwart embezzlement within the financial aspects under his or her control. By the way, if you find yourself elected as the President of the local Little League, you will find the following information to be very helpful in dealing with organizations of this type, too.

What are the *principal* places where opportunities exist for dishonesty or theft?

- The process of incoming cash and checks; the bank deposit process.

- The authorization and payment of vendor, supplier or service invoices.

- The processing of travel, entertainment or expense accounts.

- The process of receiving and shipping merchandise; the inventory control system including purchase orders; invoicing.

- Processing payroll including new hires and compensation adjustments.

- Handling of Petty Cash.

- Access to computer systems that would permit the creation or elimination of records to cover up any embezzlement.

Following is a list of specific things you can do to help prevent problems in each of these areas.

Incoming Cash.

- Someone who is not involved in making the bank deposit should be responsible for opening the mail each day. Whoever opens the mail should segregate cash and checks. Count the cash and total the number and value of checks. These totals should be given to the owner or manager before being turned over to the clerk to prepare the deposit. Each day's deposit slip should be reviewed against the control totals produced at the mail-opening step. Totals should match. If not, immediately investigate.

- Review actual cash receipts versus expected receipts on a weekly or monthly basis. Investigate variances.

- Insist on prompt reconciliation of bank statements each month. Personally review the detailed reconciliation documents. Clerks should know that the owner or manager must review and sign the bank reconciliation each month.

- Review allowances for doubtful accounts, sales returns and open account balances based on your knowledge of each account's history.

- Insist that no customer master file can be added or deleted from the computer files without the owner's/manager's prior permission. Compare counts of master files month-to-month.

- Carefully review accounts receivable aging reports each month. Look for any unusual items. Make sure the aging report totals agree to the General Ledger.

- All credit memos and account write-offs require owner's/manager's approval.

Payment of Vendor, Supplier or Service Invoices.

- Never...under any circumstances...sign blank checks!

- Keep checks under lock and key so they are not generally available.

- Use multi-part checks. One copy should be kept in numerical sequence. Check for missing check numbers at least monthly. Institute a "voided check" procedure and insist that the procedure be followed for every spoiled check.

- All checks above a certain nominal amount ($250?) should require two signatures.

- Review payable agings frequently. Be on the lookout for unfamiliar vendors or unusual items. Make sure the aging balances to the General Ledger.

- Permit no new vendor master files to be entered into the computer without your prior permission. Compare counts of the master files month-to-month.

- Minimize the use of manual checks.

- Insist that vendor invoices, purchase orders and receiving documents are matched and attached to payment vouchers or check requests (where appropriate). Review the document sets before the final checks are created.

- Use access control systems to lock out unauthorized persons from vendor and check writing systems.

- Insisting on prompt reconciliation of the bank statement helps in this process, too.

Travel, Entertainment or Expense Accounts.

- Obtain and use a standard reporting form. Insist on timely submission of the completed form with receipts for all expenditures over a certain dollar amount, say, $25.

- Insist that cash advances be closed out at least monthly. Better yet, severely limit or eliminate all cash advances.

- If company credit cards are used, make sure the credit card user knows he or she is ultimately responsible for all charges and insist on credit card receipts for each item listed on the expense report. Reconcile monthly credit card invoices to expense reports. On gasoline credit cards, check that the license numbers listed are vehicles authorized for use in the business.

- Establish firm policies regarding air travel, hotel, meal and rental car guidelines, limits on entertainment, etc.

- Personally review and approve expense accounts before they are paid.

Inventory Control.

- Consider using fenced cages for expensive components or products. Strictly limit the access to this area.

- Actual counts of units, cartons, etc., must be matched to shipping documents *before* the release of merchandise to a shipper.

- Permit no inventory write-downs without proper investigation.

- No merchandise is ever to leave the facility without an invoice or appropriate shipping document. Sometimes bosses are the worst abusers of this procedure.

- Conduct frequent physical inventories especially on "big ticket" items. Also consider using a cycle counting system.

- All employees are to exit through a single designated door at the conclusion of their work period. This should be done under the watchful eye of the owner, manager or highly trusted employee.

- Maintain a numerical control copy of all invoices and shipping documents. Check for missing numbers frequently.

- Use access control systems to lock out unauthorized persons from sales order, invoicing and shipping systems on the computer.

- Keep invoices and shipping documents under lock and key.

- Frequently inspect trash barrels to look for inappropriate scrap or discarded inventory.

- Review monthly financial statements for reasonableness of Inventory and Cost of Good Sold accounts.

Payroll Processing.

- Sign every payroll check *personally*. It may take a little time but it's worth it.

- Keep a weekly count of the number of people on your payroll. Verify the number of payroll checks against that count.

- Personally approve, in advance, every change made to the payroll master file.

- Consider a separate bank account for payroll. Deposit into that account the exact amount of the payroll. Insist on timely monthly bank statement reconciliation. Review it immediately.

- Did you sign a check for someone you can't remember? Go and find that person *now*!

- Use access control systems to lock out unauthorized persons from the payroll processing system on the computer.

- Keep payroll checks under lock and key. Maintain a numerical control system to show missing check numbers.

Petty Cash.

- Fund your Petty Cash with a workable but minimal amount of money.

- Keep the Petty Cash under lock and key.

- Every transaction should be memorialized with a Petty Cash transaction ticket.

- Insist that Petty Cash be reconciled and replenished once a month.

- Establish firm policies for the appropriate uses of Petty Cash. Restrict the use of Petty Cash funds for employees' personal use.

Computer Access Control Systems.

- As noted throughout this chapter, careful thought should be given to utilizing access control password systems on your computer system.

- Even the smallest companies now have multiple computers and LANs (Local Area Networks). Put one person in charge of maintaining the LAN. Insist on a monthly review of who has access to what, passwords or security codes in use and all devices hooked up to the LAN. Changes should be reported to you in advance of implementation and detailed logs maintained.

Security measures and control procedures will help reduce fraud, theft and embezzlement. A dedicated, resourceful thief can breach any system, however. This is especially true in small businesses and organizations where it is often impossible to restrict one person from doing many tasks. As the owner or manager, you should send a clear signal and visible message to everyone that controls are in place and that they will be diligently followed. The mere fact that you are openly investigating potential system weaknesses will discourage those who might be tempted to test the process.

On the other hand, it can be pretty discouraging to spend an inordinate amount of time "checking up" on every potential problem area. There must be a balance between prudent, consistent review of systems and controls and a basic trust that most people are honest. Only you can strike a happy medium between these two conflicting positions.

SARBANES-OXLEY; WHAT DOES IT MEAN TO ME?

Y2K was a snappy abbreviation for potential trouble. As we approached the year 2000, so-called experts predicted dire consequences in worldwide banking, public utilities, airline traffic control, government programs and other areas because of inflexible computer program designs completed years earlier. Millions of dollars were spent trying to fix the problems. Most of these disasters were going to befall us at the stoke of midnight, January 1, 2000. As we all know, nothing much bad happened and any difficulties were minor and quickly fixed.

But, 2000 and subsequent years did present us with some very difficult problems. A host of highly visible business scandals were discovered. They affected many prominent public companies managed by well-known people previously considered as pillars of commerce. While some might argue that "men have always been sinners," the egregious nature of the malfeasance, misfeasance, fraud, jaw-dropping greed and outrageous manipulation of financial reporting shocked and infuriated the investment and regulatory communities. One after another these industrial and commercial giants (and their well-known accounting firms) were forced to admit that the reported financial results were grossly incorrect. In addition, management was discovered in a feeding frenzy of personal aggrandizement collecting huge salaries, perquisites and taking enormous loans to feed their personal desire for more of everything material in life. Where were the Boards of Directors while all this was going on? In the next wave of the scandals, it turned out that most of the directors were lap dogs of senior management. Many board members were collecting fat retainers and consulting contracts and just showing up to rubber stamp whatever management proposed. Boards were not providing any meaningful oversight of financial reporting, executive compensation or other fundamental duties legally attributed to Boards of Directors. And, as previously noted, the "big" accounting firms were in huge conflicts of interest by providing once-over-lightly audits while aggressively selling lucrative consulting contracts to the same client. Newspaper headlines trumpeted one collapsing company after another. Stock prices plummeted. Investors were virtually wiped out. Employees of the failed companies often found their 401(k) plans had no value remaining. Billions of dollars just vanished. What a monumental disaster!

As could be expected, senior government legislators and regulators proposed sweeping changes in the laws governing how public companies must be operated. After endless public hearings and testimony, a package of corporate reform legislation emerged from the U. S. Congress in 2002 under the name of the Sarbanes-Oxley Act. Authored by Senator Paul Sarbanes, Democrat-Maryland, and Representative Michael Oxley, Republican-Ohio, the key provisions of the new law were:

- Created the Public Company Accounting Oversight Board to oversee and investigate auditors, including setting auditing standards, with various disciplinary powers for the rules or professional standards violations. Unlike the previous self-regulatory body, it has a guaranteed source of funding.

- Gives enhanced authority to corporate audit committees, including mandatory preapproval of many activities. Committees may have only independent directors.

- Prohibits auditors from providing various consulting and other services including lucrative financial information systems design.

- Requires rotation of key audit partners and restricts movement of auditors to the employment of their client companies.

- Mandates certification of financial reports by top executives and prohibits improper influence of audits.

- Allows companies to reclaim various incentive compensation in certain cases of financial restatements.

- Dictates that funds disgorged for securities laws violations go to a fund to compensate victims; a House Committee is currently considering a proposal to boost that fund.

- Requires enhanced disclosure of off-balance sheet transactions like those of Enron, and requires that "pro forma" presentation of financial results be reconciled with generally accepted accounting principles.

- Dictates that companies disclose whether they have a code of ethics for top executives (or why not) and any changes or waivers granted.

- Bans company loans to directors and officers.

- Requires corporate attorneys who find evidence of improprieties to report them to the CEO and/or the Board of Directors.

- Establishes new rules on stock analyst conflicts of interest, severing many links between investment banking and research functions.

- Increases penalties for securities fraud or impeding investigations, providing jail terms of up to 25 years and fines of up to $25 Million in some instances.[1]

Like similar legislative responses to perceived problems, Sarbanes-Oxley may have forced the pendulum to swing too far and will probably result in some negative unintended consequences. Any over-zealous provisions of the law will almost certainly be modified in the future. In the meantime, public companies are now faced with a whole new set of government compliance and reporting requirements that some will find onerous and all will discover to be expensive to implement. However, it was totally predictable that such a law would be passed given the scandalous conduct perpetrated by so many senior executives on every constituent group in the business community.

Sarbanes-Oxley is directed primarily at public companies subject to Security and Exchange Commission (SEC) oversight. So, what has this got to do with small and mid-sized privately held corporations? The answer may be "plenty." Many private companies find that their investors, suppliers, customers, insurance companies, banks and other business affiliates are entities who have already started to upgrade their corporate governance standards. They may expect the private companies they do business with to "clean up their acts," too.[2]

---

1. The OREGONIAN, July 28, 2003
2. The WALL STREET JOURNAL, July 22, 2003, Matt Murray, "Private Companies Also Feel Pressure to Clean up Acts."

While no one expects privately held corporations to embrace the provisions of Sarbanes-Oxley *en toto*, there are many worthwhile aspects of the law that should be considered for implementation. Some ideas just make good business sense; others may be required down the road as private companies seek venture capital, engage in possible merger discussions with public firms or prepare for an IPO. The following represent a selected group of Sarbanes-Oxley provisions that many privately held companies might find worthwhile to implement.

Composition of the Board of Directors. Most boards in small companies do not provide meaningful governance activity. Usually, the board is made up of the owner, his or her spouse, the company's outside accountant or a trusted friend. The board meets once a year (after being nagged to do so by the corporate attorney) to produce a set of minutes and appropriate resolutions for the minute book. There is no real oversight. Owners/CEOs often don't want to subject their plans or decisions to the critical input of outsiders. In fact, most owners could greatly benefit from independent advice provided by outside board members. Breadth and depth of management in smaller companies is usually limited. The owner has no one to turn to for advice, especially on matters that may be beyond his or her expertise. Recruiting and hiring independent board members and conducting quarterly meetings in depth could be a boon to many firms. Finding this new board may be difficult and costly. However, the upside potential may greatly outweigh the cost of creating an independent Board of Directors

Audit Committee. In small companies, who is looking critically at the way books are kept? Often, the owner may be reliant on a trusted bookkeeper to generate interim financial reports, some basic computer software accounting system and an outside CPA for production of year-end statements and tax returns. The in-house bookkeeper may lack the skill or training to provide meaningful financial analysis. The outside CPA is usually hired to provide year-end statements that are neither audited nor even reviewed but merely compiled from company records provided. It is often the case that small business owners do not have accounting or financial backgrounds. Standard accounting software, while very helpful to small companies, can sometimes offer inadequate audit trails and may be subject to manipulation. An audit committee of the Board of Directors could be very helpful in plugging these potential holes in the financial reporting systems. A director with financial expertise should overlook all of these systems and report potential problems to the full board.

Compensation Committee. The small business owner is fundamentally conflicted when deciding on the elements of his or her compensation. Is it fair compared to others with similar companies, duties and levels of risk? Does it appear excessive to key managers and employees? Are investors, creditors or bankers concerned with the total level of compensation? It makes good business sense to ask an independent board to assist in establishing executive compensation programs. This would apply not only to the owner but also to key managers and even lower level employees. If nothing else, the advice of the board provides "cover" to the owner when personal or management compensation becomes an issue with any constituent group inside or outside the company. "Look," the owner says, "the board carefully examined this matter and gave me specific advice. I am merely implementing what they suggested I do." If the independence and character of the board members is unquestioned their advice will speak for itself.

Certified Financial Statements. As noted above, many privately held small companies are owned and operated by people without an in-depth financial background. Over the years, they have learned how to read financial statements so as to effectively direct the company's operations. However, if asked to explain some aspects of accounting policy or financial reporting, many owners will defer to their internal accountant or outside CPA. Most outside parties like investors, creditors, bankers and others are looking more closely at privately held companies. It would behoove any business owner to give some comfort that he or she is distributing financial statements believed to be forthright. A cover letter signed by the owner should clearly state that the results provided "are a true and accurate report of my company's financial condition to the best of my knowledge." Does this type of "certification" offer some legally binding assurances to outsiders? Probably not. But, a commitment to write such a letter will force some owners to take a closer look and ask some hard questions before financials are distributed to others. This type of action on the part of the owner would definitely qualify as "good business practice."

Loans to Owners, Officers, Directors. Assume you are dealing with a small privately held company. You are this company's banker providing a substantial credit line, an investor in a minority position or a creditor with a large accounts receivable balance. You certainly don't want the debtor company diminishing cash flow by extending loans to the owners, officers or directors. We are not talking about short-term travel advances or loans out of petty cash. We're talking about companies granting large loans to their owners or officers that potentially jeopardize the cash flow of the firm. In the past, some owners might have said, "It's my company—I'll do what I want!" The days of treating a privately held corporation as a personal piggy bank are gone. Yes, there may be legitimate reasons for a company to loan money to its owner or key officers. Seeking the advice and consent of an independent board offers a rationale to outsiders who may be critical of such a loan. Not providing loans under any circumstances qualifies as another "good business practice."

Conflict of Interest Situations. Outside CPA firms not only produce year-end statements and tax returns but also consult about business systems or controls—with the same companies. Company directors are engaged by a third party to assist in merger or asset sale to the company. Personal advisors like attorneys or CPAs serve on the board. There is great potential for conflicts of interest within any organization that employs outside advisors. The message: business owners, board members and all outside advisors must be vigilant about potential conflicts of interest and avoid them. It would be good for any company to create a statement on ethical conduct and to spell out, as far as possible, the nature of conflicts that must be avoided. Chalk this up as another item called "good business practice."

Lots of small companies hope that they eventually become big companies. To achieve that objective, they may need the cooperation of venture capitalists, bankers, vendors, leasing companies, and many others. It seems to make good business sense to establish at least some of the standards required of larger, publicly held firms even before you get there. Certainly it makes the small company more appealing and easier to understand to those who may be asked to assist in the growth to a big company. All owners of small to mid-sized privately held companies are urged to consider implementing—without the requirement to do so—those aspects of Sarbanes-Oxley that can make them attractive to outside constituents.

THE NEXT STEP; PLANNING A SUCCESSION/HARVEST/ EXIT STRATEGY

Part of the American Dream is to start a business. Budding entrepreneurs can be found everyday trying to live out this dream in their own lives. New business ventures are started constantly. This happens in the face of grim statistics about the ultimate survival of startup operations. For example, 1% of all businesses fail every year and 16 of 17 startups eventually fail (according to G. H. Goldstick & Co. Tualatin, OR 2000). And yet, some *do* survive to grow and prosper, providing jobs, expanding commerce and creating wealth for the owners. Hearing about the successes of emerging businesses motivates other young dreamers. They want to try their luck at starting a business, too. They plead, "The other guy made it...why can't I?"

Quite so. Still, the average life for all corporations in the United States since 1900—giant Fortune 100 companies down to the smallest startup—is 24 years. (Dr. Lee Hausner, US Air Inflight Magazine, December 1992). This is typically the working life of the company's founder. There's an important message for entrepreneurs in that statistic. It says it's relatively easy *to get into business* but few create a plan *to get out of business* or develop a succession strategy to keep the company going. Those who start their own businesses are consumed with the work of getting the operation off the ground. They're busy dealing with financing, marketing, production, sales and administrative problems. Most of them never give a thought to "what happens next" or how their own personal game of business is going to play out. Besides, how do you get the attention of a 30-40 year old entrepreneur with the question: "What do you plan to do after you leave this business you're starting?" The usual retort is,

71

"How do I know what will happen 10, 20 or 30 years from now? I'll just work hard and see what happens."

The fact is, every business owner *will* exit his or her business some day! This exit event might be voluntary or involuntary. If voluntary, the owner may reap the rewards of many years of hard work. He or she could harvest a premium price for the business, assuring the financial future of his or her family. These resources might provide for other endeavors in life and permit the enjoyment of a future without the day-to-day pressures of running a business. A well-devised plan might create a succession strategy permitting family or employees to continue the operations. There are a variety of options available to the business owner who thoughtfully plans his or her succession/harvest/exit strategy. Alternatively, the exit from the business may be involuntary caused by a sudden catastrophe. If this involves illness or death, we often find an ill-prepared spouse or family trying to cope with the complexities of a business they know nothing about. The operation may go down the drain while the assets and goodwill of the business are squandered. Years of sweat equity and accumulated wealth can disappear in the blink of an eye. Loyal employees may be forced out of work creating suffering for them and their families. Long time vendors, customers and other service providers may be devastated over the failure of the business. The choice of *how* you will exit the business is yours. At a minimum, the business owner who plans an exit/succession strategy has a better chance of achieving his or her life's goals than those who "just work hard and see what happens."

There is a major semantic impediment to developing an effective strategy for succession/harvest/exit. Anyone can get hung up on understanding the term "exit strategy." A business owner may be in the prime of life and at the pinnacle of business success. He or she may think that "exit" means stopping work, putting his or her feet up to watch television all day or checking into a retirement community. Given this understanding, not much exit planning will ever get accomplished. "Exit" has an *entirely* different meaning. Instead of "exit" (an unfortunate word that has become the standard for describing a "what's next" strategy) think of end game planning as opening a door. You are in one space now. By opening the door, you can leave your current space and enter a new room full of interesting things. Or, think of an exit strategy like a checkers or chess game. You take several preliminary steps to position yourself to win the match and proceed to the next level of competition. Completing the game doesn't mean you can never play again. On the contrary, experience gained in one match may help you move up because of what you have learned.

More philosophically, picture yourself walking down the path described as the journey of life. There may be many side roads leading to attractive destinations. Your exit strategy is merely leaving one road and proceeding on another headed to a desirable way station. However you view "exit," avoid thinking of your planning as leading to a terminal point. Your carefully developed exit strategy should provide a new level of personal enjoyment, satisfaction and accomplishment as you continue life's journey. It is definitely not a dead-end, final destination or blind alley offering nothing for the future. Your exit strategy should be focused on acquiring the resources to accomplish a life's dream. Ever thought of taking a couple of years off to sail around the world, build a community hospital or establishing a local symphony? How about starting another business? You can do these things when you're 25 or 75! For some, an exit from the business is right around the corner. For others, it may be a long way off. Remember, *nothing stays the same.* Time drones on inexorably. The longer you delay creating a succession/harvest/exit plan, the more likely that you will leave your business involuntarily. There is no need for this to happen to you!

Visit a business owner and ask the question, "Why are you doing this?" Slightly annoyed, the owner may say, "What kind of a silly question is that? I do this to earn my living, to achieve a sense of personal fulfillment and satisfy my natural desire to accomplish meaningful work." If you persist and say, "OK, but why, *ultimately*, are you doing this?" you may be greeted with a blank stare. Most owners of small and mid-sized privately held businesses never give much thought to an exit plan. Why? For a variety of reasons. Planning is *very hard* work. Most of us hate to plan. We create elaborate rationalizations for our failure to do so. Exit planning also forces us to face our own mortality. That is uncomfortable for some of us. Most of us have a human "blind spot," too. If currently we are feeling physically well, enjoying our work and content about things in general, we tend to think that things will stay that way indefinitely. Deep down, we *know* that isn't true. But we're easily convinced that good times, good health and the overall "*la dolce vita*" will continue into the foreseeable future. It's hard to get exit planning done when we are in this reverie. It usually takes the sudden jolt of a business reversal, health concern, family crisis or some other negative occurrence to remind us that life is a series of up and down sine waves. *Whether good or bad*, we hear the message that, "This, too, shall pass away."

When should exit planning begin? If you are *really* farsighted, exit planning ideally begins just as a new business is being formed or acquired. However, most of us have too much on our plate when a new venture is getting off the ground. "End game" planning gets very little attention. There are several crucial decisions that cannot be ignored at the beginning of a new business. First, one must carefully decide on the correct corporate form. Should the company be a "C" or "S" corporation? Perhaps a Limited Liability Corporation is best. Partnerships or even Sole Proprietorship must be considered. It is vital that competent business and legal advice be sought here. And, even if an exit plan is very cloudy or difficult to discern, the business owner must factor the end game into a decision regarding the ultimate corporate or business form. Should the new business venture have more than one owner or shareholder, a thoughtfully crafted buy-sell agreement is important to the long-term health of the company. Those who band together to start a new business must have the maturity to recognize that they may not always have the same unity of purpose in the future. Multiple shareholders need to have a well-defined way of buying out an original shareholder or selling his or her shares to others. The formula for accomplishing the buying or selling must be certain, that is, not subject to last minute negotiation regarding price, terms, conditions or other contingent events. Nothing can be more harmful to a venture than a contentious battle between original shareholders who have grown apart in their values, life styles or objectives over the years. The buy-sell agreement should also be strictly applied to additional shares in the company that may be granted or sold to employees over the life of the enterprise. Even if nothing else is accomplished at the beginning of a new venture, a buy-sell agreement is the foundation of any exit plan.

What are the elements of a succession/harvest/exit plan? Generically, there are probably five. There may be more based on individual situations.

How to do it. There must be a legal and business vehicle that outlines how the plan is to be implemented. If succession within the family is involved, grooming and training of the new owner/manager must be planned and completed. An Employee Stock Ownership Plan (ESOP) is an option if current ownership wants to transfer stock of the corporation to the employees. An ESOP is a complex plan that offers both benefits and difficulties. Professional and legal advice is necessary before this option is decided upon.

Most small privately held companies do not have the opportunity to become public companies. An Initial Public Offering (IPO) is usually an option only for very successful, fast growing companies with a strong position in a visibly attractive market. While the idea of having a publicly traded company may be an ego satisfying dream, "going public" is tough, expensive, requires a management team with special capabilities and applies only to special situations.

Some companies find they are attractive acquisition candidates to other companies seeking a foothold in an industry or wishing to diversify their operations. Mergers and Acquisitions operate in an imperfect market. Buyers and sellers often have a difficult time finding one another. However, being acquired by a larger, more financially stable company for legitimate strategic reasons may fetch a premium price for the seller.

Another alternative is the Management Buyout (MBO). In this scenario, senior managers in the firm offer to buyout the interests of the owners. This is usually financed by a combination of equity investment from the buyers, outside venture capital from "angel" investors or venture capitalists and, perhaps, the seller offering some financing in the form of installment notes or other term debt. The MBO is distinct from an ESOP since not all employees are involved in the purchase. An ESOP also has a specific legal form different from a more standard agreement to purchase the stock of a company.

Finally, a succession/harvest/exit plan may include a strategy to sell the firm to an outside third party. There is an active market in the United States of people buying and selling companies. While somewhat fragmented, one can find business intermediaries in most metropolitan areas who represent themselves as brokers of business sales. It is always wise to thoroughly check references and background information before engaging any broker to sell your business.

When you begin your succession/harvest/exit plan, it is not necessary to limit yourself to any specific "how to do it" options initially. Narrow your options only after you have carefully studied the alternatives and begin to feel comfortable with the approaches that seem to work best for your situation.

Why to Do It. You should develop a clear reason for your succession/harvest/exit plan. The rationale you create may be a combination of several valid reasons. You may wish to exit in order to diversify your investment portfolio. The "Prudent Man Rule" often quoted by investment advisors says that *if more than 20% of your net worth is invested in one thing, it is time to diversify now*. Many owners of small business find that 80-90% of their personal net worth is tied up in the business they own. The other 10-20% may be in their homes. As the business becomes more successful, the risk from lack of diversification increases. This alone may be a compelling reason for exiting your business.

Perhaps you have been extremely successful and have attracted the attention of legitimate and qualified purchasers of your company. Even if these suitors arrive at a time that doesn't match your own exit plan, it is foolish not to listen carefully to their buyout proposals—especially if they are credible. You should not reject a premium offer out of hand just because it comes along at a time not convenient for you. It may be the best...and last...offer you will ever see for acquiring your company. Balance timing against your risks.

Of course, age is always a factor. With few exceptions, as we age we lose some of our youthful energy, become more interested in holding on to what we have and are less visionary about the world. Some 75-year-old business owners are still full of vigor, focused and energized by what they do each day. Others at 40 may be lethargic, burned out and anxious to be relieved from day-to-day pressure. While age must be considered, don't make decisions about exit strategy on some arbitrary number. 40, 55 or 65 are just numbers. You should be well attuned to what your body tells you about your rate of aging and general health. Annual physicals should be a routine part of your agenda. Again, debilitating health problems always happen to others, not to us. Failing to establish an exit plan just because you feel well at this moment is foolish.

Finally, the need for more challenge will lead some business owners to an exit plan. Operating the same company for 5,10 or 20 years may have become routine and boring. Moving on to something more complex, daring and exciting may hold great appeal for some that feel themselves in a rut. It's a frequent and valid reason to implement an exit plan.

How Will You Use Your Time? For someone who started out working 18-hour days, often 6 or 7 days a week, the idea of some free time is very appealing. Instead of being up at 6:00 AM, in the office working by 7:30 AM, just think of sitting at the kitchen table, having a second or third cup of coffee while leisurely reading the morning paper. Instead of going in to work every Saturday morning, picture yourself in the fresh air and sunshine watching your children or grandchildren play soccer or baseball. Instead of working all weekend long at the end of the year to take physical inventory and get the books closed, picture yourself enjoying a round of year end holiday parties, watching football bowl games and sitting by a roaring fireplace. You can easily create similar appealing fantasies in your own mind. They are all based on the following statement: "If only I had more time for myself, life would be very much better."

But, wait a minute—what if that wasn't really true? Most of us—especially entrepreneurs running their own businesses—have spent our lives on a treadmill of long hours, pressure-packed events and lonely, tough business experiences. After years of this, visualize the following scenario. Along comes a buyer who offers you a substantial amount for your company. The price the buyer is willing to pay will provide you and your family with financial security beyond your wildest dreams. The buyer also has his own management team and lets you know that your advice and counsel will only be needed for a few months after the sale is completed. Wealth and freedom are the by products of the buyer's offer. It's difficult for you not to laugh in nervous expectation for this deal to be completed. Finally, it is done and you deposit the largest check you've ever seen into your bank account. After several weeks of briefing the new managers and introducing them to your key customers and vendors, the new owner tells you, "Take some time off. I think my people have things under control. I don't believe we will have to call upon you again."

You are giddy with delight. There is a long list of things needing attention around the house that you're anxious to work on. You and your spouse have planned a leisurely motor home trip around the country. You will be visiting spots you have wanted to see for a long time. What could be more wonderful? Your financial security is assured. You have finally achieved the freedom to do what you want, go where you want and when you want without the nagging worry about running your business. If this isn't heaven, it must be close! Finally, the "to do" list has every item crossed off. The motor home trip was marvelous. You followed that up with an ocean cruise that was equally enjoyable. Now, you're home, enjoying that second cup of coffee in the morning, attending your kids' sporting events and generally taking it easy.

Why do you suddenly feel so uneasy? What is the cause of the restlessness you are now experiencing? Everything you thought you wanted in life has now been achieved (at an age where you can enjoy it) and still you're feeling miserable. An adult lifetime of working hard, smart and on the edge has abruptly been followed by unstructured leisure—and you don't know how to deal with it! You have failed to include a program of personal activity in your exit plan. Being suddenly "retired" at any age is not as easy as it sounds! A significant part of your exit plan must include how you will constructively use your newfound free time after your exit is complete. This takes a lot of careful thought and study. What do you like to do? Sure—golf, sailing, exercise and other diversions can play a part. But, you have always been productive and working. What will substitute for this all-important activity? You have a wide variety of opportunities for involvement. Depending on your interests, you might volunteer at a local hospital, deliver Meals on Wheels, be a reading tutor at a local school, help other budding entrepreneurs through SCORE (Senior Core of Retired Executives) or serve your church or synagogue. Go to your local library, university or bookstore and pick up some books on retirement. You can find literally hundreds of activities being suggested for people in your exact position. Take an inventory of your strengths, weaknesses and what inspires you. Develop a plan for using your time constructively. Failure to do this will leave you feeling insecure and unhappy. Each of us must use our time in worthwhile pursuits to achieve satisfaction. You are no exception. Don't underestimate the importance of this human need.

Defining Financial Security. Several years ago there was a somewhat amusing but extremely poignant essay in the New York *Times* Sunday magazine section. The essay examined issues related to "The Number"—defined as *that amount of money when invested at conservative rates of return that would support your definition of a 'life of leisure.'* The fundamental premise of the essay was that "The Number" differed for most people. For example, someone that had worked hard all their life in a modest job might say, "Gee, I could retire and live a life of leisure, by my standards, if I had $50,000 of annual income." To someone in that circumstance, having $50,000 coming in every year…without work…might allow them to experience a wonderful retirement filled with pleasures only dreamed about during a work-a-day life. Assuming that a 5% after tax return was a conservative rate of return, we calculate that a nest egg of

$1,000,000 would provide the desired $50,000 of annual income. (For this discussion, we will assume that the principal amount is never invaded or reduced).

To someone else who experienced more prosperous circumstances during their working life, "The Number" might be substantially higher. Again, for example, a person who worked in a high profile executive position providing significant income might say, "To continue my life style and do some of the other things I've always dreamed about will require $250,000 of annual income. That will permit me to give generously to my church and university and enjoy first class travel to parts of the world I have not seen." Using our same investment criteria, "The Number" for this individual would be $5,000,000.

You can see from these two simple examples that "The Number" would have infinite variations depending on the wants, needs and desires of any person. Here is the real question: what is "The Number" for you and your family? Investment advisors constantly suggest to us that we understand and estimate what our future needs will be. Although their calculations will be more complex and sophisticated than what we have presented, the question remains the same. What is "The Number" for you? The answer to this is crucial to your exit planning. For example, if you will rely on the proceeds of a sale of your company, what is the business worth? How did you go about establishing value? Does that value permit you to reach "The Number" you have established? If not, what kind of plan do you have in place to improve the value? How long will it take for you to achieve your plan? Is "The Number" likely to change over the period of time required to execute your plan? Have you factored in the diluting effect of inflation? Variations to these questions can be extensive. Perhaps you are willing to accept more aggressive (riskier) rates of return. Perhaps you are willing to gradually dip into your principal to help provide "The Number." Whether your situation is simple or complex, it is important for you to establish "The Number" before you can move to the next stage of your exit planning.

Tax and Estate Planning Considerations. The unforgivable sin in our society is the accumulation of wealth. There is a statute of limitations on virtually everything except success. Even the serial murderer experiences his or her own personal and final statute of limitations when the execution is administered by the state. But, if you are successful and die, even death does not get your estate off the hook. Since the inevitability of our mortality is not debatable, prudence requires that we establish a plan to deal with the estate we leave behind. Ask most people what they would like to see happen to their estate and they will say, "I want to leave it…

- to whom I want,

- the way I want,

- when I want,

- and, if possible, save every possible tax dollar I can."

If you decide to leave everything behind (that is, not give anything away) who do you want to leave it to? Most people will decide to leave it to their children, grandchildren or other family members. They vaguely understand that the government is going to confiscate a certain portion of the estate but that is inevitable. Be clear about this: without proper planning, the government is going to take *a lot* of your estate!

Recently revised tax laws will result in a diminishing tax on estates up to the year 2010. Currently, the law has a "sunset clause" that is effective at that time and taxes will revert to previous levels. No one can have a crystal ball in the volatile political environment we are now experiencing. However, I feel comfortable in asserting that politicians will always find a way to tax success at the time of a person's death. So, while my assumptions may be modified by current legislation, the concept is probably accurate even if the math needs to be updated.

Let's examine the simplified example of a person who founds and builds up a business that is eventually sold for a capital gain of $10 Million. Without proper planning what would be the net bequest to a grandchild? Examine how the principal might be taxed (this is a generalized example):

Sale of the company above its tax basis	$10,000,000
Federal and State Capital Gains taxes	($2,900.00)
Balance of estate tax at death	$7,100,000
Inheritance Tax, 1st Million at 55%	($550,000)
Inheritance Tax, balance of bequest at 75%	($4,575,000)
Net proceeds to grandchild	$2,075,000

Wow! Can this be true? You bet it can (depending on the current estate tax laws in effect) especially if you do not seek competent, experienced counsel to help you deal with this problem. While many people have wonderful children or grandchildren, you will often hear folks say:

- "I don't want to ruin my kids by giving them too much money."

- "I made it on my own; let them make on their own."

- "There will plenty left over even after all the taxes are paid."

- "I don't want to take incentives away from them."

- "My kids don't know how to manage money anyway."

So many people decide, by default, to leave the bulk of their money to their *first born child*—the government. After all, the *first born child* often needs more help than the others, knows how to spend money better and has not received enough help from you during your lifetime. So, if you do nothing to fix the situation, your *first born child* will...

- take what you have,

- give it to whom he wants,

- the way he wants,

- when he wants,

- and, if he can, maximize the payment of every possible tax dollar.

Many fall into this horrible trap for any number of indefensible reasons. Some will say, "I'm too conservative; the plans you suggest are too complicated." Others will say, "The plans suggested are too aggressive and, besides, I'm against paying professional fees for this type of advice." Some will just say, "I just don't like the word 'irrevocable'." Finally we hear, "I would rather just do nothing and let the tax system decide." That will insure that your *first born child* will have a field day with the money in your estate

There are four principal methods of reducing estate taxes:

- Planning evaluation,

- Fractionalizing ownership,

- Discounting the future value of gifts, and

- Freezing estate value.

Most of us have heard of some of the tools used to reduce estate taxes. But, few of us (and I include many lawyers, CPAs and estate planning professionals) know how to use the following techniques to lower estate taxes. Either singly or in combination, one needs to consider how each of the following could assist in reaching our major goal of leaving our estate to whom we want, when we want, how much we want and, if possible, to minimize the amount of taxes paid.

- Living Trust.

- Marital By-pass Trust.

- Credit Shelter Trust.

- Qualified Terminable Interest Property.

- Qualified Domestic Life Insurance Trust.

- Spousal Resource Trust.

- Personal Residence Trust.

- Qualified Personal Residence Trust.

- Business Trust.

- Children's Trust.

- Grantor Retained Income Trust.

- Grantor Retained Annuity Trust.

- Charitable Retained Unitrust.

- Charitable Remainder Unitrust.

- Charitable Remainder Annuity Trust.

- Charitable Lead Annuity Trust.

- Grantor Deemed Owner Trust.

- Beneficiary Deemed Owner Trust.

- Family Limited Partnership—Class One, Class Two, Class Three.

- Limited Liability Family Corporation.

- Installment Notes.

- Installment Gifts.

- Self-canceling Installment Notes.

- Private Annuities.

- Dynasty Trust.

- And more!

This list is not intended to impress you that the author knows a bunch of "secret" ways to avoid estate taxes. Nor does the author have the expertise to apply these methods and techniques to the variety of situations that could be encountered. Just as the score is not the music, the road sign is not the journey and the menu is not the food, merely knowing about these techniques doesn't help. I'm suggesting that knowledgeable specialists can employ a wide range of methods to assist someone with accumulated wealth to legally avoid the payment of some estate taxes. Will the resultant plans be complicated? Yes. Will those experts who know how to develop these plans using all available techniques charge a fee for their work? Of course.

Time and again, I encounter business owners who deeply regret their failure to establish a succession/exit/harvest strategy early in their careers. Some find themselves needing to exit their businesses for any number of reasons. However, their failure to plan has left them unable to execute an exit strategy due to current circumstances. While that may be painful, every situation usually possesses some seeds of resolution. The key point is: *If you haven't begun working on a succession/harvest/exit strategy yet, begin now.* Even a delayed plan will permit you to solve some of the exit issues. Adopt the following mantra: "Nothing stays the same." It will assist you getting started on your plan today.

THE HARVEST EVENT; HOW TO MAXIMIZE THE PROCEEDS

Whether we like it not, every business owner *will* exit his or her business some day. It would be great if everyone developed detailed plans for how this exit was to occur. In most cases, no planning is done. Many business owners forge ahead day after day operating the business as best they can. Little thought is given to that day when it will be desirable—or necessary—to dispose of the business. The actual disposition of the business can take many forms. These include creating an Employee Stock Ownership Plan (ESOP) through which the company's employees effectively purchase the shares of the owner. Other forms of disposing of a business can be a merger with another company, turning over ownership to children or other relatives, liquidating the assets of the business or selling the business and/or its assets to a third party. Regardless of which vehicle is used, we are speaking about a harvest event when, hopefully, the business owner will receive adequate consideration for all the hard work, "sweat equity" and value that has been built up in the business over the years.

While there are a variety of forms available to dispose of a business, we will concentrate on the sale of the business and/or its assets to a third party. This is probably the most common form of business disposition. In addition, a discussion of the process of selling a business touches on almost every aspect of disposing of a business in other ways, too. Four major topics will be addressed: How to value a business, the exit process itself, deal structure considerations, and negotiating strategies. Volumes have been written about each of these issues. This chapter is intended as a "tops of the trees" review of these topics.

For the serious inquirer, a community or college library will provide many additional sources on the subject.

Many owners of privately held businesses fall into traps when they begin the process of exiting their business. It's easy to make mistakes. For most people, selling their business is a once-in-a-lifetime event. It's likely that a business owner has little experience with this task. Unfortunately, a mistake in this process can be disastrous. Selling a business is often the largest economic event of one's life. It has enormous financial and life style implications. Obviously, the business owner wants to do everything possible to avoid the minefield of problems he or she will face while disposing of the business.

What are the most *common* mistakes sellers make? Three things come to mind.

- Selling the business for less than it is really worth.

- Selling to the wrong buyer.

- Selling at the wrong time.

It is surprising how often each of these mistakes is made. Successful, highly experienced business people who are smart, shrewd and confident commit these errors. Why? Mostly because owners of privately held businesses think that selling a business is just like selling a home or a car. The comment is often heard: "I've sold lots of home and cars over the years. Selling a business can't be *that much* different." Well, *it is!* There are many places to get tripped up. The first of these is the valuation of the business.

Selling the Business for Less than it is Worth.

Consider this scenario. You've decided it's time to sell your business. How much should you ask for it? You wouldn't think of selling a car without checking the "Blue Book." You wouldn't sell a home without talking to real estate professionals. The same can be said for selling a business. *You must find out what the business is worth…what is its value?* How is this determined? Typically, three methods are often employed to value a business.

- Let's say you approach a friend in your service club who recently sold a business. "How did you go about valuing your business," you ask. The reply: "No problem! I just used a P/E ratio that was average for companies in my industry." We all know that P/E ratio stands for "Price/Earnings" ratio. In other words, the *price* of the company is some multiple of the *earnings* of the operation. While that may apply for public companies that are subject to substantial scrutiny by regulatory agencies, it doesn't necessarily work for privately held companies. That's because many business owners make a career of legally reducing earnings in their companies in order to minimize income taxes. For many companies, we find there may not be much "E" in a P/E ratio. This is a flawed approach to valuing a privately held company.

- Perhaps we can ask our accountant to help us value the business. He or she is highly competent and has served us well for many years. Ask your accountant to value your business using generally accepted accounting principles (GAAP) and he or she will tell you that value is defined as the difference between your Assets and Liabilities. In other words, GAAP accounting says your business value is the Net Worth on your Balance Sheet. What about all the intangible assets your company possesses—customer lists, distribution channels, patents, trained personnel, etc.? Don't they count for anything? Not using GAAP. How many business owners would sell their successful businesses for its Net Worth? Not many, unless there were unusual circumstances. This is another flawed approach to valuing a privately held business.

- If you're a member of a trade or industry association, you might check with the association's Executive Director. Companies in most industries are bought and sold all the time frequently using industry "formulae" that have been developed over time. These formulae are usually some multiple of revenues, profits, number of employees, etc. The problem with these industry multiples is that they are *averages*—defined as "the best of the worst and the worst of the best." Most business owners would not describe their company as "average." When you use averages to value your business, you may short-change yourself two ways. First if your business is *above average*, you will undervalue your company and leave chips on the table. Second, if your business is *below average* you will overvalue your business and it probably will never sell. This is another flawed approach to valuing a privately held business.

In fact, none of these generalized valuation approaches will get the job done properly. Even the Internal Revenue Service says these are not the best methods of valuing a privately held company. The IRS has published Revenue

Ruling 59-60 which clearly spells out the methods to be used for valuing a private corporation. One thing the IRS makes clear: No "formula" approaches are permitted in the valuation process. Naturally, different methods will apply in varying circumstances. Of all the approaches spelled out in IRS Revenue Ruling 59-60, those dealing with *estimated future earnings* seem most promising. In other words, the real value of a company is based on the *future* of the company. Does that mean that historical financial performance of a company has no weight in valuing a business? Of course not! We *do* want to know how the company has performed operationally in the past. We also want to know what net asset values have been accumulated over time. (See attached flowchart depicting a methodology for valuing a company). However, the major factor in valuation is *what will the business do in the future.*

Think about this. When you are considering a personal investment, you're naturally interested in how the stock, mutual fund, etc. had performed in the past. But, you are much more interested in estimates of how it is going to do in the future.

The same idea applies to valuing a business. The seller of a business will prepare, say, three years of historical Income Statements, Balance Sheets and Cash Flow Statements to show how the company has performed financially. More importantly, the seller must produce credible projections showing what the future of the business can be. The future of the business has *much more* effect on value than what has happened in the past. *This is a key point.* Failure to focus on the future of the business will often result in a seller leaving chips on the table.

Now, just about anyone can do some projections showing future revenues, earnings, cash flow, etc. All one needs is a personal computer and some current spread sheet software. The problem is how to make the projections credible to an outside third party. To achieve credibility requires careful research into the macro and micro indicators of how your general industry and specific business might do in the future. This is referred to as "market research." While market research might not be the forte of most business owners, there is often substantial data available about trends, projected future events and similar information that can be assembled. Make sure you know your company's SIC (Standard Industry Classification) Code. Using that, you can track down all available information within the U.S. government. Try the Commerce and Labor Departments first. Of course, scan every trade publication for data that appears relevant. Get on the Internet and search for information about your industry and the geographic market area where you operate. Check with local colleges and universities, too. They often try to provide their graduate students with an opportunity to work with companies in "live" situations. You may be able to get some eager, enthusiastic assistance from a team of young, bright students for a very modest cost. Also consider retaining a market research firm to develop the data needed to make your business projections credible. What you must do is provide the backup data that renders your financial projections believable to an outside party who might be interested in acquiring your business. No one has a "crystal ball" to predict future events. However, it is much easier to convince a skeptical outsider about your estimates of the future if you have assembled some solid evidence to support your position.

The attached flowchart shows that many other steps are required. "Recasting" historical Operating Statements and Balance Sheets is another significant task. To recast means to restate financial statements to show *what the business would have looked like had it been operated as the division of a publicly held company*. As noted previously, many owners of privately held companies will make financial decisions that would not be considered in a division of a publicly held company. For example, the owner of a business might pay himself or herself a salary in excess of what a public company might pay a general manager to run a similar sized operation. Perhaps the private company employs family members who might not necessarily be retained by a public company. Company cars might be provided in a private operation, not in a public division. The list of these potential differences can be extensive. In most cases, a side-by-side comparison of a private company and a division of a public company with similar revenues and gross margins will show the public company to be more profitable. Remember, the private company will often do all it legally can to avoid taxes. The seller of a private corporation needs to show a potential buyer what the historical financial profile of the company is without being burdened by these anomalies. Recasting emphatically *does not* mean trying to deceive a potential buyer.

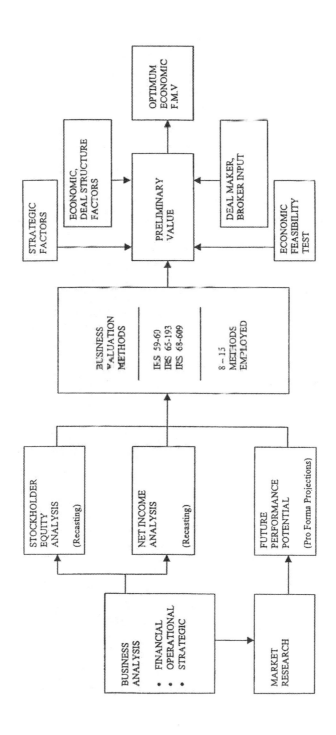

VALUATION METHODOLOGY

When recasting financial statements, the seller *always* shows actual book numbers, any recast amount (with a detailed explanation footnoted) and the revised figure. Recasting applies to the Balance Sheets as well as Operating Statements. A review of asset and liability accounts of a private company will often reveal items that would not appear on a public company Balance Sheet. Such items as Loans to Owners or Notes Due to Owners are two examples. Others might include Fixed Asset accounts that are artificially low because of aggressive write-offs to the Operating Statement. This could affect a buyer's view of Depreciation and the implications for improved Cash Flow under new ownership. The above treatment of recasting is much abbreviated. While this discussion is limited, the actual work of recasting is most important and requires careful, thorough review.

Recast historical financial statements and credible projections provide a foundation for the valuation process. Additional work is necessary to complete the task. First, one must examine external factors that might increase—or decrease—the value of a business. What intangible assets does the company possess that could be of great strategic value to some buyers? What aspects of the company's operations add value even though they may not show up on the financial statements? Is the company of special interest to foreign investors because of unique distribution strength or channel position? There is a long list of factors that can materially increase the value of a business beyond its financial statements. The seller and his or her advisors need to investigate every possible option to assure that the maximum valuation is determined. Second, one must check for the reasonableness of any valuation model. This is referred to as a valuation "high water mark" or "sanity check." There are many merger and acquisition publications that display the values of completed deals. A prudent seller will study this data to make sure his or her valuation model has produced a reasonable result given the facts available. In the final analysis, the valuation of a privately held business is *much more art than science*. Lacking a public market to value the company's shares, the owner(s) of a private corporation must assemble as much data as possible, seek competent outside advice and finally make a judgment about the value the business. Failure to do the hard work, to look beyond historical financial statements and to carefully assess the value of the company's intangible assets often results in undervaluing the business. This means the seller will leave chips on the table when the harvest event, or sale, actually takes place.

Selling the Business to the Wrong People.

The second common mistake sellers make is to sell to the wrong people. Who to sell to seems so obvious to most sellers. The logical people to approach about buying the business are either your biggest, strongest competitor or your own employees, right? In both cases, the potential buyers know a great deal about the business, require a minimum amount of transitional time with the seller and clearly understand the growth opportunities for the business. However, if a seller turned to a competent business broker for advice, both groups of potential buyers would probably be far down the list. Here's why. In most cases, a competitor is not interested in paying a premium price for the business. He may wish to acquire some key customers, talented employees or certain product lines. He really doesn't want most of your company. After all, he probably has the same deadbeat accounts you have and the same inventory that you haven't been able to sell is on his shelves, too. No, what he really wants is to "cherry pick" the best parts of your business and discard the rest. That will seldom result in a premium price. What about selling to employees? (This does *not* refer to an ESOP). While there may be good superficial reasons, selling to employees is often a bad idea. In most cases, employees do not have the financial reserves or borrowing power to take on the purchase of a business. Therefore, the seller would probably have to accept poorly collateralized notes for the bulk of the purchase price. This can create constant stress worrying about the ability of the former employees to successfully operate the business so that the notes will be paid off. Like the potential competitor buyer, the employees don't want to pay a premium for the business either. Because of their "insider" position, they expect the seller to give them a bargain price. There are also potential legal issues when selling to employees. Check with your attorney about recent cases of "fraudulent conveyance of assets" when businesses have been sold to employees. You will hear some chilling stories.

A word about selling the business to your children. How many children pay a premium price to their parents for the business? Probably none unless they structure a highly leveraged transaction. When the kids do that they must often commit the capital needed for future growth to the purchase. They wind up struggling with working capital and short of resources needed to grow just to pay off the parents. Mom and Dad, are you really doing your kids a favor by selling them the business? Perhaps not. Consider the possibility of gifting to your children some portion of the purchase price. Tell them, that when the business is sold, you will pass on a "stake" for them. They can use this to start something for themselves. This may be a better solution for both them and you.

So, if kids, competitors and employees are out, to whom can you sell you business? It won't take you long to find that there are many buyers in the market looking to acquire sound, prosperous businesses. In the Merger and Acquisition (M&A) circles, it is often said that there are at least ten qualified buyers for every good deal. This raises two questions: How do I find these buyers? How do I qualify them? You can run "blind" ads in the *Wall Street Journal*, New York *Times*, Chicago *Tribune*, Los Angeles *Times* and similar publications both in the United States plus London, Tokyo, Hong Kong and other major foreign cities. You will probably get a slew of responses but they will be totally unqualified. You will have to do a lot of work determining which responses are legitimate, fully qualified buyers. Another approach is to make contact with some M&A firms who act as intermediaries between buyers and sellers of businesses. Almost all of these M&A firms have prequalified buyer databases listing companies and individuals who are seeking businesses to acquire. This information does not come for free. M&A firms will want you to engage them, for a fee, to assist in the sale of your business. It is often a good idea to hire someone to help you in this process. After all, it takes a lot of time to complete a sale of a business. You're so busy running your business, do you really have the time to devote to this task? There is also a question about the seller's competence and lack of experience with this type of transaction. The key task you face in selecting the right company is to thoroughly check out their track record. Find out how long they have been in business and how broad an area they cover. Contact the several references you ask them to provide. Don't engage any business intermediary until you clearly understand what they are going to do for you and how much the entire process will cost. Also check as many references as possible. Satisfy yourself that you're putting this major economic event into the hands of those who are trusted and competent.

You should also develop a list of buyers you believe could have a strategic interest in your company. Strategic buyers will frequently pay a premium price compared to a financial buyer. The strategic buyer may be an offshore company who wants to enter the U.S. market and sees the value of your distribution network. The strategic buyer may be a company associated with your industry. They may be making acquisitions to vertically integrate their company...and you fit in. Even if you retain an M&A firm to represent you, this list will be a good prospecting file for them. As you prospect for buyers, *do not* limit your search to domestic companies. Almost every good business that comes on the market will be attractive to offshore buyers. For a variety of reasons, foreign companies will often pay a substantial premium to acquire a U.S. company.

Selling at the Wrong Time.

The third common mistake is selling at the wrong time. Many business owners will say, "I'm going to sell out when I'm 55," or, "I'm going to exit when my net worth is $2 Million." These statements imply that the seller is in control of when he or she will sell the business. Almost nothing could be further from the truth! The fact is *you will achieve the maximum harvest for your business when the market lets you!* This timing has nothing to do with your age or current net worth. General market and business conditions, interest rates and other economic factors will be the key determinants of when you will exit your business. If you set arbitrary time constraints on your exit, you may be disappointed. What if you plan to leave at age 55 only to find the economy is "in the tank" and there is virtually no M&A market? No, you must constantly monitor the economy and market situation. You may achieve your maximum harvest value before— or after—some arbitrary birth date or net worth objective previously set. Don't be afraid to leave early if you can see that the financial portion of your exit plan can be fulfilled. There is one crucial thing to remember when is comes to successfully harvesting a business. *Timing is everything!*

Avoiding the three common seller mistakes will help to make the job of successfully harvesting your business easier. Before proceeding to the next major topic, we must address another aspect of the harvest process that can get a seller into a lot of difficulty. It will sound like an issue that could be easily avoided. Unfortunately, human nature often gets in the way. Many of us have a strong desire to talk about what is going on in our lives. The sale of our business is often such an important event that we're anxious to share our progress with others.

Confidentiality.

Almost nothing will kill a potential deal faster than a breach of confidentiality. A seller in the final stages of transacting a sale of the business must recognize the urgent need for secrecy. There are numerous documented stories about deals destroyed by failure to maintain confidentiality. The problem usually develops because the seller feels the need to inform a lot of people about his or her impending plans. Everyone from long-term key employees, lawyers, accountants and other advisors *seem* to have a "need to know." Often, this is simply not true. *To the maximum extent possible*, a seller should keep the details of a harvest event to himself or herself until the last possible minute. Lawyers and accountants are normally not needed for preliminary planning except in a general way. Employees, even the most trusted and loyal, will surely begin asking, "What will happen to me?" if they know about the pending transaction. Many sellers assume the source of potential "leaks" will be the buyers. This is rarely true. Most buyers are eager not to have their acquisition plans known. They are as eager to maintain confidentiality as the seller. So, here is a key tip presented in blunt language…keep your mouth shut! There are enough problems associated with completing a deal. Don't make the mistake of letting a breach of confidentiality get into the mix.

The second major topic to be addressed is the exit process itself. The detailed method of your exit may take one of many forms. Included in the alternatives for exiting are "going public" through an Initial Public Offering (IPO); merger with another company; disposing of the company through some form of Charitable Remainder Trust; establishing an Employee Stock Ownership Plan; or, a sale to a third party. As mentioned previously, our discussion will focus on the last mentioned option.

While every rule has exceptions, the evidence indicates that the successful sale of a business usually takes between nine and fifteen months, twelve months on average. During that time the seller will invest 800-1,200 hours of time working on the selling process. Exiting a business successfully is a relatively long, tough job that consumes great quantities of energy both physical and emotional. It's worth saying again that the sale of a business is often *the largest economic event* in a person's life. If the process results in a maximum economic harvest for the seller, then it is time well spent. Each seller must be willing—and able—to devote this kind of time to the task. If not, one must consider how to find outside assistance with all, or some parts, of the process.

Many standard Merger and Acquisition (M&A) theories postulate that there are thirteen specific steps one must complete to successfully sell a business and achieve a maximum economic harvest. Can any of these steps be avoided or by-passed? Probably, but short-circuiting the process could result in a less favorable final result. Following is a discussion of these thirteen points.

Starting the Process. This may sound silly but it's something you must do. You need a firm decision to get the process underway. This is often the biggest—and hardest—decision a seller will make. It implies that a ball is rolling that cannot be stopped. While that's not necessarily true, it does signal that a very significant event has been initiated. The decision to go forward is the first step in the selling process.

Determining the Value. A seller must determine the value of his or her business. As discussed above, this is a combination of historical financial performance and future projections supported by credible market research. There are a number of good computer software packages that can assist with number crunching and presentation. You may wish to engage a professional business valuation expert to help you with this task. Remember, your value to a strategic buyer may be markedly different than to a financial buyer.

Decision Point. After determining the value, you may decide to go forward with the process or to stop now. Obviously, if the valuation produces a number lower than your expectations, you may not wish to go forward. However, you have not wasted any time or money obtaining this valuation. If is too low, you now have a road map showing what you must do to increase the value. A thorough valuation, updated yearly, is a wonderful management tool for any business. Alternatively, if the valuation is pleasing to you, a decision can be made to continue the process.

Develop and Exit Plan. A formal exit plan should be established for each individual who will be affected by the sale of a business. (Please refer to the chapter in this book, "The Next Step.") A spouse running the business needs an exit plan. The spouse who may not be involved in the business day-to-day nevertheless needs an exit plan, too. Selling the business may dramatically alter both of their lives. In general terms, an exit plan spells out what you are going to do with your time and your wealth after selling the business. It should address tax issues, a review of family and/or insurance trusts, and an examination of documents such as wills, health care powers of attorney and similar legal matters. The plan must also specify how one plans to spend his or her time and energy after exiting a business. After you have left your business you will find that there are a finite number of things to fix, paint or remodel around your home. You can travel only so many times around the country in your motor home. After awhile, even ocean cruises can become boring. Think hard about "what's next" in your life. If you are exiting at an age when real retirement is appropriate, fine. But, if you still have dreams to dream and mountains to climb, make sure you figure out how to accomplish those things. Part of your plan may be to continue working for the company you plan to sell. Most sellers are required to stay with the company for a transition period with the buyer. A carefully crafted exit plan establishes important elements of any deal structure. Exit planning, while vital, is also difficult. Coming face-to-face with our own mortality can be uncomfortable. A key point to remember: *Nothing ever stays the same*. An exit plan helps us to document that ultimate fact.

Creating a Marketing Plan. If your company planned to introduce a new product or service, you would surely develop a detailed marketing plan. Who are my target market prospects? Where are they located? What kind of literature or brochures do I need? How and where will I advertise what I have for sale? How do I "roll out" the product or service across the country—or the world? What are the features, advantages and benefits of my new product or service? In *exactly* the same way, you must create a marketing plan for the sale of your company. Selling your company won't just happen. You need a carefully crafted plan to insure the successful completion of the task.

Develop a "Brochure." Qualified and sincere buyers will want to know a great deal of information about your company. This data must be arranged so that your acquisition opportunity can be evaluated thoroughly. Whether or not you receive a bona fide offer depends on the completeness of your "company resume" or offering memorandum. The exact structure of this information can take many forms. Following is a representative Table of Contents that covers most situations.

The Purpose for the Document

An Executive Summary

    The Seller's Motivation for Selling

    Historical Highlights

    Future Opportunities

Products and Services

    Product Descriptions and Branding

    Product Mix

    Pricing and Gross Margins

    Industry Growth Information—Historical, Future

Markets and Customers

    Market Share Position

    Customer Mix, Geography and Concentration

    Account Potential

Sales and Marketing

    Sales Channels Employed

    Advertising, Promotion Strategies

Suppliers

Competition

    Major Competitive Firms

    Barriers to Entry

Company Organization and Administration

    Historical Background

    Corporate Form, Ownership

    Key Employees and Staff

    Litigation or Potential Contingent Liabilities

Facilities

Financial Analysis

    Summary

        Revenue

        Profitability

        Cash Flow

    Historical Financial Schedules and Notes (at least 3 years)

    Pro Forma Financial Schedule and Notes (probably 5 years)

    Exhibits and Notes

If you do a good job preparing your company brochure, it will probably be 20-30 pages in length. Your particular situation may call for a longer—or shorter—version. Some sellers will include a video showing facilities, equipment or their products in application. Your objective is to tell a qualified potential buyer just about *everything* regarding your company. This is no time to hide anything. Negative information will almost surely come out as a sophisticated buyer examines all the facts. Should a potential buyer uncover something he or she feels you tried to withhold, you lose a great deal of credibility and run the risk of jeopardizing the deal. So, tell the truth. It will come out in the long run anyway.

Develop a Summary Marketing Document. Would you want your major competitor to see the document described above? Of course not! The company brochure/resume/offering memorandum should be reserved for *seriously* interested buyers who have been *thoroughly qualified* in advance and have signed a non-disclosure agreement. To be qualified, a potential buyer must present verified financial credentials permitting them to complete a transaction near seller's estimate of value. There is a need, however, for a summary marketing document that can be used to develop prospects for the sale of your business. Typically this document will describe the general industry, summarize major financial highlights, speak generally about staff, facilities, potential, etc. This document may be only one or two pages in length. Often this summary is "blind," that is, it does not specifically give the company name, location or other information which could directly identify the business. The summary document is mailed to the target companies shown in your marketing plan. Here is a point where assistance from a business broker can be valuable. Mailing to their database of qualified buyers, or specific sub-sets, may broaden your marketing effort. Ideally you will wish to send out 500-700 summary marketing documents to potential buyers.

Prospecting and Qualifying. When you send out 500-700 summary marketing documents two additional forms are also sent. The first is a Confidentiality Agreement sometimes referred to as a Non-Disclosure Agreement. The second is a request for detailed financial references. The potential prospect is advised that, if further interested, he or she must execute the Confidentiality Agreement. It must be returned along with detailed, verifiable financial information about the person or entity that may actually be the purchaser. Very often potential buyers will ask the seller to provide detailed financial information before the buyer will commit to being interested in a possible transaction. *This is exactly backwards.* The seller should know, in advance, if a potential buyer has the financial strength to be considered as a serious acquirer. Once this has been established and a Confidentiality Agreement has been executed, the seller may consider the buyer to be both serious and qualified. If you distribute 500-700 summary marketing documents, you may expect that 5-10 prospects will emerge as financially qualified and sincerely interested buyers. These are the people to whom you can send a copy of the company brochure/resume/offering memorandum.

The Negotiating Process. This document presents many important points about selling a business. The following may be the most important thing you will read: *To maximize the harvest from the sale of your business, you must have multiple buyers in the negotiating process simultaneously.* If you are dealing with only one prospective buyer, *he is in control of the situation*, not you. This process, called a Limited Auction, is absolutely crucial to obtaining a premium price for your business. The Limited Auction can be conducted with high ethical standards. It should not be considered as "playing one buyer off against another." You are merely saying to the potential buyers, "Look, there are several other buyers who have the same facts as you. If you are seriously interested, please take your 'best shot' since we will compare your proposal to all the others." This will assist the seller in establishing a maximum exit value and a sense of urgency among potential buyers. Without a Limited Auction you *cannot* maintain control of the negotiating process. Some buyers will refuse to participate in a Limited Auction. They know that this process favors the seller and they don't want to lose their position of control. The seller should eliminate these buyers from consideration even if they are otherwise strong and attractive companies. Please remember: *One buyer is no buyer*!

The negotiating process itself is often grueling, hard and stressful work. Both parties are trying to put together a deal they believe is most favorable to their side. Obviously, this can result in a lot of tension, harsh words and emotional ups and downs. The two sides will try to obtain agreement from their adversary on a wide variety of issues. Some will be accepted easily, others will require protracted give-and-take. There will be more about negotiating strategy later. The key element of the seller's negotiating strategy will be determined by the exit plan described above. It will provide a detailed blueprint for what the negotiations should produce for the seller.

The Letter of Intent. The key purpose of the negotiating process is to produce a Letter of Intent. In laymen's terms, the Letter of Intent is an agreement to agree. The basic Letter of Intent (LOI) can normally be written in 2-3 pages. (This can be considerably longer if third party financing is involved). In its simplest form the LOI states the price to be paid, the terms of payment, the conditions that must be met by both seller and buyer to close the deal and the time frame for getting the transaction completed. One condition normally insisted upon by the buyer is that the seller "standstill" for a certain length of time. This means that the seller will not negotiate with others during the "standstill" period. This is a reasonable request. However, the seller should insist that this period not be extended since he or she doesn't want other interested buyers to opt out of the process for too long.

The Due Diligence Process. Once the LOI is executed, the buyer will immediately move to complete his or her Due Diligence. This is a legal term that essentially means the buyer will carefully verify all the facts presented to him or her in the company brochure/resume/offering memorandum and in the negotiating process. This is often the most dangerous time for any transaction. In today's culture, questions related to past or current litigation, environmental problems, unfunded pension liability, workers compensation cases, inventory valuation and product liability issues might quickly become "deal killers." Sellers are urged to carefully and honestly respond to all reasonable requests for information from the buyer. The very worst case scenario involves closing a deal only to have the buyer subsequently discover negative information that was withheld by the seller. This may be a cause for an action of fraud and the unraveling of the entire transaction.

The Definitive Purchase Agreement. The Definitive Purchase Agreement (DPA) is the legal document upon which the transaction will be closed. Even in the smallest of deals the DPA can be quite voluminous and contain many side agreements, schedules, transfers of leases and titles, etc. Who drafts the DPA—the buyer's attorney or the seller's attorney—is always subject to debate. If the buyer arranges for the first draft, the seller will have to negotiate out many onerous clauses…but won't incur the legal costs to prepare the document. Conversely, a seller's attorney will draft a more "friendly" document but the seller will have to absorb the cost of this legal work. There is no easy answer to this dilemma. However this is resolved the DPA should be the first time you require the services of an attorney on an extended basis. Many sellers rely upon legal counsel to negotiate the deal. This can be a mistake. Lawyers, by training, are adversarial. What you really want from your legal counsel is two things. First, you want to properly memorialize the business agreements you have reached with the buyer. Second, you want to craft the DPA with the legal language that provides the highest level of protection to you in the future. While the seller probably missed some of the legal "niceties" in the negotiations, you should count on your counsel to put those things into the final documents.

No matter how thick the DPA becomes, the seller *must* focus on the section entitled "Representations, Warranties and Indemnification by the Seller." Normally, the heart of any transaction is condensed in this part of the document. Even though the seller is not a lawyer, he or she must understand the implications of this section of the DPA. The hardest, most intense final negotiations almost always occur over the terms of representations (what the seller states to be fact), warranties (what the seller guarantees to the buyer) and indemnification (the financial assurances given by the seller related to future potential damage to the buyer). As the seller, *make sure* you clearly understand what you're agreeing to in this section.

The Closing. This is the easy part, right? Not necessarily. The Closing is a fairly formal ritual normally held in the office of one of the attorneys. Prior to the Closing ceremony, a pre-closing checklist is managed by one of the lawyers to insure that all the documents needed to close are properly assembled. While it is assumed that everything is in order and agreed to, this may not be the case. The parties involved review each and every set of documents signing or initialing where required. Often, new issues are raised during the Closing that require additional negotiations. This may require strikeovers on some documents and preparation of new agreements, etc. Unless there is a monumental blowup the Closing is finally completed. The two principals exchange documents, cashier's checks and a handshake. The deal is finally completed. Spelled out in a document like this chapter, the entire process sounds quite logical and progressive. In the real world, all transactions related to the sale/purchase of a privately held company seem to have a life of their own. Every deal I have ever seen is full of intense emotion, produces euphoric "highs," incredible "lows" (where suicide becomes a viable option) and sucks energy and vitality out of every participant. Of course, there is a great sense of relief when the deal is finally done. However, there is one final word of caution. Look out for both seller's and buyer's remorse. After all the smoke has cleared, many will be heard saying, "Why in the world did I do this?"

There are the thirteen steps of the selling process. Can you skip some? Maybe, but you do so at your own peril. Remember, selling a business is usually a once in a lifetime event. You will only get one chance to do it right. Don't screw it up!

We turn our attention to the deal structure itself. There are several forces that will determine the final structure of the transaction. Do you want to stick around and continue working in the company for awhile? Is this an asset or stock sale? (Depending on your corporate form, this can make a big difference in the taxes you pay). Are you seeking all cash, or as much cash as you can get? Are you interested in some cash combined with a payout that provides an extended earnings stream? What advice have you been given regarding the tax implications of the deal? The list of considerations is virtually endless. Every transaction is unique. The buyer's and seller's needs must all be addressed and satisfied to the maximum extent possible or the deal won't happen. Nobody gets everything they want. In the final analysis, the transaction must be "win-win" or it won't fly. As you reach the end point of negotiations, you will find that there may be some really serious issues—"deal killers"—that have to be resolved. Following is a short list of current matters that can wreck a deal. If you have some of these present inside your company, be prepared to handle these issues.

Unresolved or Pending Litigation. Just about everyone is concerned about the prospect of a "bottomless pit" lawsuit. Buyers don't want to inherit this kind of a problem. You may be required to offer a significant amount of indemnification.

Environmental Issues. Anything that looks like it could attract the EPA is a very serious matter. Be prepared for a demand that you provide an independent clean bill of health if your company has ever been involved with underground tanks, plating, metal finishing or foundry operations. The same is true if you have ever used solvents, distillates, etc., in your production processes.

OSHA. If you have ever gotten on the Occupational Safety & Health Administration radar screen, expect to provide exquisite detail about how you have corrected safety problems, potential work hazards or dangerous production processes.

Pension Plan Funding. If you have an existing pension plan, make sure you can document that it is fully funded both now and into its actuarial future.

Adequate Insurance. The issue extends not only to property and casualty but also to general liability and, more importantly, product liability. If you're insured on an "occurrence" basis, what about potential claims from products sold prior to the sale? This is a very serious issue to the seller.

Inventory Accounting. This is the "granddaddy" of all deal breakers. Expect very hard negotiations regarding the value of the inventory transferred at the time of the sale and how any future problems will be indemnified by the former owner.

To list all potential "killers" poses too exhausting a task. Be aware that you must face them and, ultimately, deal with them successfully or you won't close a deal. I'm sorry to tell you—again—that the process of selling a company in a manner that generates maximum value is complicated and arduous.

An important part of the deal structure considerations is how you will be paid when you sell your company. There are many forms of consideration and several almost always used in combination to satisfy the seller. The final consideration will be dependent upon what you can negotiate, your tax situation and the unique elements in your deal. Some typical methods of payment, along with a brief commentary, are noted below.

Cash. Most of us are very familiar with these green, rectangular pieces of paper adorned with pictures of our Presidents. This is a desirable form of consideration. However, it is important to know that an "all cash" deal will almost always be the lowest price that the company can fetch. If the seller is somewhat flexible about the up-front cash, he or she can usually negotiate a better overall price for the company.

Stock. Many sellers take stock in the buyer's company. Naturally, you would never take stock in a privately held company since there is not public market. Unless you have firmly guaranteed buy-sell arrangement or an iron clad "put" option at a favorable price, you are advised never to accept stock in a non-public company. Sellers should even be wary of stock widely traded on a major national stock market. What protection do you have against a severe drop in value? Accepting stock is risky and should be carefully evaluated.

Convertible Debentures or Bonds. A bond or debenture is a collateralized promise to pay a certain amount, usually with interest, at a specific time. Make sure the collateral is adequate, the interest rate is fair and the time to maturity short enough for your purposes. A convertible debenture is a bond that may be converted to an equity instrument, like common or preferred stock, under certain conditions and at specific times.

Notes from the Buyer. There are horror stories told at every country club and service club meeting by people who sold their businesses and took back a note from the buyer as a major portion of the consideration. With variations, the hapless sellers tell of not being paid and then incurring legal fees to regain possession of their former companies. If and when they are successful they find that the assets have been raped, customers have turned elsewhere, employees are all gone, goodwill has evaporated—in short, they repossess a pile of ashes. They discover that they didn't *sell* their business—they *rented* it to an unscrupulous buyer. It doesn't have to be that way! There are at least five specific ways to secure a note from a buyer in addition to the stock of the company he or she will offer the seller as collateral. The five methods:

1. Demand a personal guarantee secured by outside collateral such as a home, raw land, etc.

2. As part of the note, insist that no company assets on the Balance Sheet (as of the closing date) may be sold without your express written approval in advance.

3. Restrict the compensation, both direct and indirect, that the buyer and his family may take out of the business until the note is paid off. In other words, starve him to death until you're paid.

4. Demand that he or she provides you with monthly financial reports *sent via the U.S. mail.* Why the Postal Service? Should the reports be fraudulent and sent through the mail you may go directly to Federal Court for relief without waiting.

5. Insist on a seat on the Board of Directors until you're paid off. The buyer does not want you sitting on his or her Board and reviewing every decision. It is a further incentive to get you paid off—and out of the way.

Royalty or License. This method can be an effective way of increasing the overall purchase price. It works especially well if you are close to introducing a new product or service that you believe will be very successful. By taking a royalty on sales, you may obtain a lot more consideration in the long run. Similar points can be made about licensing some of your technology instead of selling it outright.

Consulting Fees. You probably have valuable knowledge or contacts that the buyer wants transferred to him/her. You may structure part of the purchase price in the form of a consulting contract that guarantees an income stream for an extended period of time. Be aware that this method may result in negative tax consequences for you since the fees are Ordinary Income.

Employment Contract. You will almost surely be asked to stay with your former company for some period after the sale. During this transitional period, you should negotiate an employment contract that cannot be canceled except for the most grievous types of action. One caution: Make sure any employment agreement is a separate legal document from the Definitive Purchase Agreement. You may soon find out that you just can't work for a "boss" anymore. Should *you* wish to break the employment contract, insure that this issue is dealt with as an entirely separate legal matter. If the employment contract is an integral part of the overall agreement, an attempt on your part to terminate the employment deal might trigger an unraveling of the whole transaction.

Non-compete Agreement. You may be asked to agree not to compete with the buyer of your company for a specific period of time and/or in a certain geographical area. This is a reasonable and customary request. Make sure you are compensated for keeping your part of the bargain.

Earn Out. The seller should always consider an Earn Out as a bonus on top of the purchase price. An Earn Out allows the seller to be compensated for future growth in earnings or profits. If you are confident in the future of the business and will be around to help "make it happen," you may wish to negotiate for an Earn Out. This can be an excellent way to get a premium on the sale of the business. It is a mistake to include the Earn Out in the basic consideration paid for the company.

There are many other forms of consideration. For example, some people will negotiate for a new car every two years for the next ten years. For others, a season ticket to a favorite sporting event or theatrical series is important. Some may want special medical coverage for a seriously ill spouse. A wide variety of consideration options exist. The development of a detailed exit plan will determine the key elements of consideration sought by the seller. Since each exit plan is unique, the exact form and mix of consideration elements will be unique to your situation.

The fourth of our topics is negotiating strategy. First, a few comments about some key principles of negotiating. Most entrepreneurs consider themselves to be excellent negotiators. They have spent their business careers putting together deals for leasing facilities, vendor terms, union contracts and customer orders. The sale of a business, however, requires entirely different negotiating skills. First, the seller is often dealing with a professional buyer who acquires many companies and is very familiar with the process. Second, the sale of one's business is often wrapped up in your life's work. Over the years, your company has become a part of the fabric of your life. You're not selling a business—you are disposing of a part of you. In other words, selling your business can turn out to be a highly emotional event. *When emotion enters, logic and clarity often leave.* All sellers are advised to get some professional help, at least with this part of the sale. You're only going to get one chance to get it right. Someone who possesses objectivity about the negotiations should lead the negotiating effort with the buyer.

There are three specific negotiating concepts that warrant discussion.

Establish Value/Price. There is a big difference between *value* and *price.* Knowing the value of your business is crucial. So, how do you deal with questions about price? In almost all initial discussions between seller and potential buyer, the buyer will get around to asking, "So, how much do you want for the business?" If the seller tries to be coy, the buyer will persist and use many different approaches to ask the same question. "What is it going to take for us to get a deal done?" Unless he gets an answer, the buyer will finally say, in exasperation, "Look, if you won't give me your asking price, how do you expect me to respond to you?"

In spite of this insistent pressure to put a price on the table, every seller is advised to heed the following advice: *Under no circumstances should you tell the potential buyer how much you want for your company.* Instead, your response should consistently be, "Mr. Buyer, it would be presumptuous of me to tell you how to place a value on my business. You may have an entirely different view of the value from mine. What I will do, however, is to give you all the information about the company so you can determine what it might be worth to you." If you place an asking price on the table, it can be guaranteed that *you will never get one single penny more than that price.* The asking price will become the place where negotiations begin—and it will always go down from there. You can clearly see the beauty of having multiple buyers looking at your business simultaneously. Multiple buyers will keep each other honest. They will be reluctant to "low ball" a price since you can then politely say "no" as you usher them out one door while inviting the next buyer in with a different offer.

Establish Urgency. One tactic of buyers is to stall and drag out negotiations once they are underway. By doing this, the buyer believes time is now working for him. The delayed negotiations may drive away potential rivals. It can also wear down the seller on price, terms, etc. From the outset, the seller needs to state clear expectations for the pace of negotiations. Let the buyer know that if he or she is responsible for delays in the process, you will terminate negotiations and move on to other options. It is up to the seller to keep the negotiations on track. The buyer is right—time is almost always on his or her side.

Establish Terms. The shrewd seller will create a two-part "wish list" for the negotiations. Part One is the list of non-negotiable demands such as the minimum acceptable price, the rock bottom amount of cash consideration and other seller required terms. The seller must be clear that failure to achieve everything on the non-negotiable list means walking away from the deal. Part Two is everything else that would be *desirable* to obtain through negotiations. This list may be very long and represents the issues that, if obtained, would provide "whipped cream on top of apple pie." The order of negotiating these two lists is crucial. The seller must always conclude the negotiations on Part One of the list before moving to Part Two. One technique of negotiation is to "give up" certain points to your adversary in exchange for other things you want. If you have constructed your two-part list properly, you can afford to give up most or all of the points on Part Two so long as you have gotten everything you want on Part One.

There are many techniques in the negotiating process. Libraries are full of books written on the subject. The following comments relate to several important points.

Meeting Agendas. Never attend a negotiating session that does not have a detailed written agenda. You should always know, in advance, subjects to be discussed so that you can be properly prepared. It also prevents you from being "ambushed" on a subject you don't want to cover in that meeting.

Documentation. Take detailed notes of every meeting. Summarize your notes in a memo to all participants. This will help to flush out your adversary who may wish to talk a subject to death but never reach agreement or concede your point. Nothing speeds up negotiations like well-documented meetings.

Package Yourself. If the potential buyer wears a suit and tie, then you do likewise even though that is not your normal dress. Insure that the location for the meetings is businesslike and conducive to work.

Manage Your Advisors. You must stay in control of the process yourself even if you are not physically present in the negotiating room. Make sure that you are not abdicating any of the important decisions to your professional advisors. All too often, small business owners turn to their accountants, attorneys or consultants to make a crucial decision about a potential sale. This is almost always wrong! Yes, you should solicit their expert advice. But no one knows more about what you want than you do! Don't let someone else make those "calls" for you.

What conclusions can be drawn from this presentation about a harvest event...selling your company for maximum value? The following ten points provide a good summary.

1. Your business may be worth more than you think. Many business owners are limiting their options because they don't know the value of their business. If you know the value you can be much wiser about setting a course of action for the future. Do you know the value of your business?

2. You *will* exit your business someday. The implication of this is that you must begin planning—today—for your eventual exit from the business. Without an exit plan, you will find yourself vulnerable to the fragile vagaries of life. Make sure you are in a position to exit your business on your terms.

3. To know the value of your business is the first key for any agenda. No decision about selling or continuing is really possible until you have a

good idea about the value of your business. This issue must be resolved before anything else can be considered.

4. You must document the value of your business. Impeccable documentation, properly supported by credible market research, is the only way you can convince a skeptical outsider about the real worth of your business. Don't skimp on this part of the overall selling process.

5. You must have a clear idea of your own objectives. Have you clearly spelled out what you want from the possible sale of your business? Have you committed this to writing?

6. You must be in control of the selling process. The key factor is to have multiple buyers looking at your company. Remember, *one buyer is no buyer*. Only by dealing with more than one buyer concurrently can you maintain control over the negotiations.

7. The price for your business will be determined at the negotiating table. Obtain good advice for this stage of the selling process. Don't make the mistake of thinking you can negotiate the final deal on your own. Sellers frequently leave chips on the table—or worse yet, kill a really good deal—when they try to accomplish negotiations on their own.

8. Timing is everything. Be careful not to set some arbitrary date for exiting your business based on age, net worth, etc. You will receive the maximum harvest from your business when the marketplace tells you that the time is right.

9. Remember, there are always external factors at work. Many of the things that will determine the value of your business and the possible timing of a sale are totally outside your control. Make sure you are attuned to these factors.

10. Understand your risks. When you started your business, your major investment was probably in sweat equity. Now, you have grown the business into a prosperous, thriving operation that has considerable worth. Had the business failed in the beginning, all you would have lost was some time and a little money. Now, however, your business is worth real dollars. Constantly assess the risk you run by continuing

to operate your business. Keep asking yourself, "Is it time—now—to harvest my business?"

The American dream of owning your own business can turn into the American nightmare if a proper exit strategy is not developed. Prudence tells us to understand the inexorability of time. Take the time—right now—to begin working on your own exit/harvest strategy.

SUMMARY; CAN A SMALL COMPANY BE GREAT?

We have heard the old axiom, "Knowledge is power." It would be more accurate to say, "The *use* of knowledge is power." Knowing lots of stuff is not very helpful unless you put it into action. This book has addressed eleven specific issues faced by small business owners. At one time or another these situations will probably affect most companies. It certainly is not an all-inclusive list of problems owners will encounter. If we addressed every item that came across the business owner's radar screen, this would be a very long book indeed. I have tried to focus on some big issues. There is (to me) a logical progression in the chapters. Chapter 1 talks about starting a business. Chapter 11 addresses the harvest event. In between, I speak about how to improve corporate governance, borrowing, financial controls, cash planning and similar situations that can dramatically affect the overall value and direction of a small enterprise. Two side bar chapters about fraud and Sarbanes-Oxley were added because they are timely.

I hope the readers of this book are eager to make their small companies not just good but great. Jim Collins, in his wonderful book "Good to Great" says, "Greatness is not a function of circumstance. Greatness...is largely a matter of conscious choice." I highly recommend a thorough reading of Jim Collins' book for anyone seeking to build a great organization or company.

Can your small company become great? I don't know. But, if Jim Collins is correct, any greatness you achieve will follow your conscious choice. You can choose to do the right things with your company from beginning to end. Following the chapter order of this book, I offer a summary of the things I think you need to do to make your small company great:

- From the very outset of your enterprise, don't skimp on the organizational and legal aspects. As the business gets off the ground, everyone will be busy trying to secure financing, developing customers, outfitting a new facility, hiring key staff and a doing a million other things. It is easy to ignore or put off dealing with the proper corporate form, buy-sell agreements and possible exit strategies. All those topics sound like they are issues for the future. They're not! I can relate case after case where clients have said to me, "If only I had handled these things at the beginning. Now, it's ten years later and I'm faced with a difficult situation that will be very expensive to solve." Time is your enemy when a business is being launched. In spite of this, you must find the moments to deal with the issues spelled out in Chapter 1. You'll be glad you did.

- Clients have told me, "I'm too busy running this business to spend time with Boards of Directors or Advisory Committees." Corporate governance is a central issue throughout the life of any company. The owners must figure out a way to leverage their own talents. Often the principals will have little or no skill related to leading their little company into a big, successful company. They rely on their own abilities and sometimes are blinded to important issues that can lead to later problems. I have observed several cases where an effective Advisory Committee has helped to make a struggling company a thriving and successful operation. Don't make the ego-centered mistake of thinking you have every skill necessary to run your company. Spend some time to find a mentor, create an Advisory Committee or establish a truly objective Board. When you find the right people and convince them to help you, life will instantly get better for you. Sure, to make outside advisors effective requires work on your part. But it can be well worth the effort. Review Chapter 2 and begin a plan to get creative about your corporate governance.

- Insuring that any company has the right amount of financing in place is a continuous task. There is never a time when a business owner can sit back and say, "All my financial dials are properly set. I now can go out and just execute." Every business is dynamic; events can change monthly, weekly or even hourly. Am I appropriately financed right now? Could I attract new funds if I needed them? Do I have the right mix of debt and equity on my balance sheet? What does my current bank think of me? The majority of small businesses will never be able to attract the large pools of money controlled by venture capitalists or merchant bankers. Therefore, it is important to understand how you can obtain commercial or bank credit. Chapter 3 spells out what most bankers look for when deciding to loan money. You will also see how much you might be able to borrow based on the collateral you have available. Set aside a certain amount of time every month to cultivate lending sources. In addition to your own bank, it is prudent to stay in touch with other lenders as well. Remember the banking axiom: always arrange for funding well in advance of when the money is needed.

• I have often been asked if there is a central problem with my small business clients. My answer is easy. Most small business owners do not know how to read "the scoreboard." In other words, they do not clearly understand how their operational decisions affect the financial performance of the company. Many owners are brilliant engineers, marketers, sales people or manufacturing wizards. Too few of them have much of a financial background. Don't misunderstand; I'm not trying to fill the world with accountants. Just like a game of football or baseball, you really can't tell what is going on or who is winning without reading the scoreboard. The "game of business" is like that, too. Owners need to gain enough accounting and financial knowledge so that they can understand the key elements of their "scoreboards." Chapter 4 recommends a program of what to keep track of in your business. You will also find some suggestions about key ratios to monitor and how an owner can keep current on a daily basis. Make sure you're spending enough time reading the "scoreboard" so you will know if you're winning "the game of business."

• If our bodies are denied sufficient blood, we can die. If our lungs do not get adequate oxygen, we can die. If our companies do not have enough cash, our businesses can die. Cash is the blood and oxygen of any business. No matter how brilliant your marketing, how superior your product or service or how solid your customers, your business can expire without cash. And yet, most business owners do not know how to calculate the cash flow in their business. Bankruptcy courts are full of companies who just completed the largest revenue year in the history of the operation. Why? Because the operation outran the ability of the owner to supply adequate cash to handle the growth. Chapter 5 speaks in simple terms about how to calculate your cash flow. Since cash is so crucial to business existence, you are well advised to know as much as you can about how to calculate the cash requirements of your business.

- Most small business owners do not have sophisticated financial systems in place. They think that they will be unable to do analysis like the big companies do. That's not always true. There are many effective techniques to provide the small business owner with tools to help him or her run the business better. Chapter 6 is a mini-chapter explaining how to do some basic breakeven analysis. While not very nuanced, it does provide a helpful way of determining what to do when potential problems arise. Take a look and see if you can't find some useful information in Chapter 6 to assist you in running your small business.

- A small business is started and before long it is growing and prosperous. One of the first issues to face the business owner is expansion to a larger facility to accommodate growth. Chapter 7 provides important information regarding the following dilemma: Should I lease or buy my new facility? Many people will fail to examine their alternatives because they are not flush with cash. It may be, however, that the economic situation is right to borrow enough to own a facility. Examine this chapter again for the details about how you can calculate what a building might be worth and how to obtain a loan to construct it or buy it yourself. Even if conditions are not present for you to build or buy your own facility, you will learn how to examine the alternatives available to you.

- When your company is small, you are often limited in administrative staff. One person may be responsible for the bookkeeping while handling the company's cash, paying its bills, processing its payroll and maintaining most financial records. You will often be blest with a loyal, hard working and conscientious employee who is scrupulously honest. You must be aware, however, that the *opportunity* for fraud and embezzlement is always present when a handful of staff processes all the company's financial transactions. Chapter 8 provides some specific approaches to discourage fraud and embezzlement in your business. The suggestions are easy to implement and will go a long way toward keeping you free of this ugly problem in your operation.

- There are many reasons to maintain a company as privately held. The lack of scrutiny by public agencies and the legal and accounting savings associated with being private are two of the biggest reasons. Over time, a small company may grow larger and more powerful. The business begins to appear on the radar screens of industry leaders, large financial institutions and prominent customers. It may be important for the business to act much like its publicly held competitors. Big customers, lenders and suppliers may expect the privately held company to follow the same ground rules as public companies. It is often very good policy to adopt some of these rules even though the private operation is not legally subject to their provisions. Chapter 9 spells out some of the ways the current federal law concerning corporate and Board behavior might help the privately held concern. Provisions of the law, referred to as Sarbanes-Oxley, can actually work in favor of the small or midsized privately held corporation. Check it out.

• Most owners of small businesses do not have a well defined succession plan or exit strategy. Part of this problem relates to the word "exit." Most people think of this as a terminal point when you leave the business, put your feet up and watch daytime TV for the rest of your life. Nothing could be further from the truth. A well crafted succession or exit plan can help drive the company to attain specific goals over a fixed time. Without this type of planning, most companies tend to drift in a commercial river. They are unprepared when the river turns into a white water rapid and then a waterfall. It is foolish to tie an exit or succession plan to some fixed birthday like 40, 55 or 65. Successful exits can be made at any age. Chapter 10 guides you through the process of thinking about exiting a business. It is one of the major issues to be faced by the owner of a privately held business. Failure to properly plan can result in severe negative consequences.

• You have done your best. The business you started some years ago has prospered and grown. The exit planning you have done is in place. Now is the time to turn over the business to someone else. The reward for this turnover will be financial success allowing you to retire, follow your life's dream or start another new business. Selling a business to someone else can be a perilous experience. Chapter 11 outlines the specific steps you can take to maximize the proceeds in the sale of your business. The chapter also discusses valuation issues, how to negotiate successfully and how to make sure you stay in control of the selling process. You will also find a discussion of the biggest mistakes seller's often make during the process. By emulating the success others have had when selling their businesses and avoiding the mistakes made by some, you can expect a successful experience when it is time for you to sell your business. Remember, selling a business is usually the most significant economic event in your life. You must get it right.

I'm unsure if reading this book will allow you to reach Jim Collins' definition of a great business. After all, it's up to you although I am willing to be a cheerleader for your success. I do believe that I have provided a number of knowledge kernels that can assist you in operating your business better. Each chapter deals with an issue that I have personally faced or has been dealt with by one of my clients. Since the *use* of knowledge is real power, I hope you take what you have learned in these pages to help make your business prosperous, personally fulfilling, a great place for people to work and an admired company.

ABOUT THE AUTHOR

Greg Hadley has had a distinguished 46-year business career. He served 10 years with IBM, was General Manager of Computer Sciences-Australia and operated several private companies. Since 1990, Hadley has advised 110 private Northwest firms. His prior book, "Fundamentals of Baseball Umpiring," is displayed in the Baseball Hall of Fame.

SELECTED BIBLIOGRAPHY

Bruce Blechman and Jay Conrad Levinson
Guerrilla Financing—Alternative Techniques to Finance any Small Business.
Boston, Houghton Mifflin Company, 1991

William D. Bygrave and Jeffry A. Timmons
Venture Capital at the Crossroads.
Boston, Harvard Business School Press, 1992

Dickson C. Buxton
You've Built a Successful Business—Now What?
Glendale, CA, Griffin Publishing Company, 1996

James C. Collins and William C. Lazier
Beyond Entrepreneurship—Turning Your Business Into an Enduring Great
Company.
Englewood Cliffs, NJ, Prentice Hall, Inc., 1992

James C. Collins and William C. Lazier
Managing the Small to Mid-sized Company—Concepts and Cases
Chicago, Richard D. Irwin, Inc., 1995

James C. Collins and Jerry I. Porras
Built to Last—Successful Habits of Visionary Companies
New York, Harper Collins Publishers, 1994

Jim Collins
Good to Great
New York, Harper Collins Publishers, 2001

Sidney Davidson, Clyde P. Stickney and Roman L. Weil
Accounting: the Language of Business, 4th Edition
Glen Ridge, NJ, Thomas Horton and Daughters, Inc., 1979

Deloitte, Haskins & Sells
"Raising Venture Capital; An Entrepreneur's Guidebook"
1987

David M. Dodson, Stanford University Graduate School of Business
"Cash Flow Analysis" (a teaching note)
1988

Gary Goldstick
Business RX—How to Get in the Black and Stay There
New York, John Wiley & Sons, 1988

Erich A. Helfert
Techniques of Financial Analysis, 4th Edition
Homewood, IL, Richard D. Irwin, Inc., 1977

Paul Hawken
Growing a Business
New York, Simon & Schuster, Inc. (Fireside), 1987

Charles T. Horngren
Introduction to Management Accounting, 4th Edition
Englewood Cliffs, NJ, Prentice Hall, Inc., 1978

Bryan E. Milling
"Cash Flow Problem Solver"
New York, Chilton Book Company, 1984

Wesley J. Smith
"Should You Incorporate?"
Home Office Computing, September 1994

Thomas J. Martin and Mark Gustafson
Valuing Your Business
New York, Holt, Rinehard and Winston, 1980

United States Small Business Administration
"Understanding Cash Flow"
1994

J. Fred Weston and Eugene F. Brigham
Essentials of Management Finance, 5th Edition
Hinsdale, IL, The Dryden Press, 1979

0-595-32769-9

Printed in the United States
134501LV00016B/53/A